Theme-
Centered
Interaction

To Jetta,
Tamar,
and Eve

MYRON GORDON

with the collaboration of
NORMAN J. LIBERMAN

Theme-Centered Interaction

AN ORIGINAL FOCUS ON COUNSELING AND EDUCATION

NATIONAL EDUCATIONAL PRESS
711 St. Paul St. - Baltimore, Md.

First Edition

International Standard Book Number: 0-87971-004-7
Library of Congress Catalog Card Number: 72-76599

 National Educational Press, Inc.
711 St. Paul Street
Baltimore, Maryland 21202

Printed in the United States of America

Preface

Especially with first-born books and children the author and parent are engrossed in the act of exploring both the product and their interaction with it. I began this book five years ago, enthusiastically carrying the brand of the theme-centered interactional approach to therapeutic and educational group workers. The energy I derived from the fantasy of being a sort of standard bearer happily sustained me through these years when there was no reliable signal that my efforts would bear fruit. I saw my job as bringing the theme-centered inter- actional method into the mainstream of other parallel group approaches while establishing its place and identity in the group work family. My own style of learning and teaching was to guide group workers from other disciplines in gaining a comprehensive grasp of TCI, including its historical and methodological connections with other theories and procedures.

I found myself at first down in the basement at a ping pong table piled with books and notes from my past. In this warm room with the furnace blower breathing a pleasant screen of sound, I produced — in a cognitive and thinking state — much of what is written in Part One.

At this time my friend and teacher Ruth C. Cohn was of great help to me. Originator and developer of the theme-centered interactional method since 1955, Ruth was undoubtedly the one best person to communicate the essentials of this rich new approach. As a frequent group member and co-leader with her in workshops conducted by the Workshop Institute for Living-Learning in New York City, I gained a grasp of this new method through intensive experiences. We exchanged many ideas. Her perch was in my attic, where she was so lulled by the buzz of family life sounds drifting upwards that she uncovered new writing talent which had been muffled within herself for many years.

Up to that time only Ruth Cohn had written — rather briefly — about the philosophy, structure, and process of TCI, frequently known as the "WILL" method. I asked Norman J. Liberman, my friend and colleague and one of the chief architects of TCI, to help me in the complex task of defining the new approach (or "system" as we sometimes thought of it when considering its encompassing quality). His indispensable contribution is woven into the book. The concepts of mode, elaborations of the meaning of theme and descriptions of the various processes in TCI terms (in Chapters VIII, IX and X) are Norman's original formulations.

In practice of what we preached, Norman and I had our own two-man living-writing workshop. It has been the master vehicle of our work together. It rescued us when ideas ran dry; when beset by pleasurable and painful distraction; when with conflicting personal tendencies we had to cross over to each other or be lost.

A source of energy flowed from my ongoing professional activity. On the faculty of Queens College counseling students and teaching counseling, I was given the freedom to introduce this new TCI approach in my daily work. I can explain this rare opportunity to experiment not only as my doggedness in convincing the administration but also as a savory result of the enlightened policies of the

Honors Program and the Departments of Student Personnel and Education. In this era when the experiential and encounter spirit is expanding to permeate professional, social, and personal life (reminiscent of psychoanalytic influence in the second quarter of the century), I found ways on the college campus of integrating some of the best features of the analytic and the experiential in TCI workshop and classroom formats.

The TCI method is a synthesis of group procedures along many continua. It is aimed at balancing the cognitive, conative, and affective, one or another of which has become overemphasized or neglected in existing group approaches and in daily living. The TCI method emphasizes the experiential while inviting authentic communications for both leader and participants. Ruth C. Cohn[1] describes it as:

> "a small group in which each individual is encouraged toward autonomous achievement of concentration on the preannounced theme as it develops in the group's inter-action. Simultaneously, attention is directed toward intra-psychic and interpersonal awareness of the total self and the group, as well as . . . distractions from the theme . . . Each person, each I, is encouraged to state himself at any given moment: what do I want to get from and give to this group? The get-and-give is related to me, to you, and to the theme, and includes the progressive forward search and re-gressive holding on to the stagnant — that which I knew before."

Each individual is asked to concentrate on the announced theme as it develops by group interaction. In the light of the theme, the leader and group members work toward intrapsychic and interpersonal awareness of the total self and the group. The focused theme is definite in its referent, but open-ended. Thus the words "leadership in groups" constitute a good *topic*. But a theme needs the added impetus of the active, self-stating process. Therefore "Being Myself and Becoming a Leader," once stated, enters the thought processes and associations of participants. The experience of several people responding to one theme is heuristic for productive cohesion in a group. In the TCI method focus does not mean blinders. People become free to share personal responses to the central theme with awareness of and in interaction with others doing the same thing. As in chamber music a high value is placed on

[1]Personal communication.

making room for the others' solo parts and on attending to the ensuing dialogue. The desired result stems from a dialectic of *letting it happen* — meaning other voices — and *making it happen* — meaning speaking clearly of one's own experiences. The leader exercises his judgment, intuition and timing in developing and integrating these processes.

By virtue of its ground rules and design, the TCI approach has built-in machinery for involving the total person. One example of how it works is "speaking for I." This phrase is not a quirk of grammar — or even a brand new idea — but a principle which leads into genuine interaction around a theme. Instead of speaking for "children" or for "people who live in rural areas" or for "women," a participant speaks for himself, about his or her experiences with particular people.

What we have just illuminated are three elements which are present and worked with in the group at all times: the I (individual), the We (group), and the It (theme or purpose). The personal and interpersonal openness and honesty, together with the cognitive quality of the TCI experience, become the cumulative tradition of the group, resulting in a contagion of healthy interaction and shared learning.

This volume is for group counselors and other group workers who have already mastered some of the beginning principles and practices of working with individuals and groups. In an identity crisis of his own, the responsible group worker tries to find his way in the forest of group guidance, group therapy, and group experience. There are other puzzling issues. Is he trained to do what is expected of him? Does his own perception of professional role conform to the perception of others in the school, agency, and community? Is he to have education, guidance, counseling, and dynamic, experiential, and therapy groups all at once, or one at a time? Is there a model of group work which provides the necessary flexibility, depth, and scope to absorb the many innovations now being advanced? Group workers need answers to these questions.

Our purpose is to provide a system which can be integrated with practice in education, guidance, counseling, and psychotherapy in groups — and which will satisfy the broad spectrum of requests for service in an era of social uncertainty and changes. Members of the Workshop Institute for Living-Learning have already functioned at two extremes of a social spectrum: at one end in group consultations with large, "establishment" corporations and school systems and at the other end with "East Village nomads," casualties of our changing youth culture.

In Part One the theme-centered interactional method can be seen and appreciated in perspective through an exposition of counseling, group dynamic, and group therapeutic theory and practice. This opening is followed in Part Two by an extensive presentation of TCI. In Part Three we point to possibilities for directly applying and integrating this method with educational and therapeutic groups. Part Four is a sound recording of an unrehearsed workshop, illustrating many of the principles and practices of TCI.

One pleasure in using this method has been stirred by the realization that TCI has its immediate and natural use in unexpected situations. To take a common example, imagine grumpy members of a family, waking up tired and irritable on a Monday morning. While not advocating a full-blown TCI workshop to get people up and around in such a predicament, I can think of a small-scale TCI effort. Let us view these parents and children as aiming toward being autonomous and interdependent members of a family. Upon awaking and getting ready to leave the house, not only did they lack a common "theme," but they were hobbled with a series of individual disturbances. We could provide a theme, such as "Starting to Face the Day in My Family." This might have served at breakfast to mobilize effort toward a common and positive goal. Granted, this example does not quite have a broad or original sweep; I wish only to indicate here that TCI has everyday applications wherever people are concerned.

How to explain why I asked so few people for assistance? One rationale is my working style. I frequently built as I went along with only the most general blueprint in mind, permitting fleeting ideas to crystallize into sections and chapters. In this case it was good for me to rely on "inner help." Also the writing "workshops" shared with Norman were effective both in expediting our task as well as in providing the leaven of an experiential interaction. On occasion, Sondra Heller provided her very special editorial competency.

I must not forget my friend, Leo Goldman, of the City University of New York, who came forward when I called upon him to give his gentle but incisive comments on parts of the manuscript.

Myron Gordon, Ph.D.
Queens College, CUNY
Flushing, N.Y. 11367
December, 1972

Contents

4: The Sounds of a TCI Group

(Audio cassettes with accompanying notes)
Eleven participants share their actual group experiences with the listener, in an unrehearsed workshop with the theme "Experiencing and Evaluating the Theme-Centered Interactional Approach." The session covers the workings and implications of this method in schools, families and other settings.

Hymn to the United Nations

Eagerly, musician,
Sweep your string,
So we may sing,
Elated, optative,
Our several voices
Interblending,
Playfully contending,
Not interfering
But co-inhering,
For all within
The cincture of the sound
Is holy ground,
Where all are Brothers,
None faceless Others,

Let mortals beware
Of words, for
With words we lie,
Can say peace
When we mean war,
Foul thought speak fair
And promise falsely,

But song is true:
Let music for peace
Be the paradigm,
For peace means to change
At the right time,
As the World-Clock
Goes Tick and Tock.

So may the story
Of our human city
Presently move
Like music, when
Begotten notes
New notes beget,
Making the flowing
Of time a growing,
Till what it could be,
At last it is,
Where even sadness
Is a form of gladness,
Where Fate is Freedom,
Grace and Surprise.

—W. H. Auden

1

Anchorage

I

The
Search

The quest for uniqueness and identity in the counseling function produces five elements: *content, process, human development, self of the counselor,* and *integrative effort.* The order of these five categories stands in no special historical sequence. Each element deals with specific aims and procedures which are considered intrinsic to the emerging profession of guidance and counseling. Some of the writings presented here reflect the influence of older roots of counseling; others are related to present-day educational and psychological theories as well as to future developments. To preserve the style of each author, this chapter lets the proponents of different schools of thought speak in their own voices. After each section the reader will be shown the connections of these five elements with the theme-centered interactional method.

Stress on Content, Cognition and Directiveness

In the beginning there was *content*. Frank Parsons' innovation in 1909 was that he brought together knowledge of man with information about occupations. From then on the guidance movement was concerned with testing, evaluating, diagnosing, orienting, transmitting, and teaching this information in the best possible way to the student. Masses of significant facts about the educational process and the learner soon provided guidance workers with useful information to share with students, school personnel, and parents. This accumulation of content provided the counselor with much of what he needed in areas of educational and vocational guidance. The weight of these essentially cognitive procedures carried over to personal counseling. The wealth of available content related to "mental health" and interpersonal relationships challenged many counselors to devise methods of sharing these important intellectual insights with those whom they counseled. Ellis (1962) has developed a comprehensive system based on a rational-emotive approach.

Bennett's (1963, pp.242-244) suggestions for examining the self-concept provide a sample of many possibilities for "content counseling." A group was asked to communicate about the question "What am I like?" She referred to Cooley's method of having an individual compare his own picture of himself with what others think of him and, finally, discuss his image of himself in the future. In still another approach a counselor guided a student to write a composition concerning ambition, strength of reality awareness, attitudes toward self and others, worries and tensions, self-directiveness, and development of a serviceable life philosophy.

Content can become overheated and boil over. Frequent exceptions to this tendency are the bull sessions among students — taking up as many hours a week of education as courses — which seem to have built-in safeguards against disorganizing hostility and anxiety. Most often the purpose and result are supportive and cohesive. But we have seen ill effects of unstructured and undirected informal "marathons," leaderless groups, and "Who's Afraid of Virginia Woolf" sessions at parties.

Samler (1965) cautions about slipping too readily into the content of pathology. He states that the schools have gone too far in stressing mental health approaches which even begin to mirror the "formal therapeutic situation." The school should now depart from its Freudian preoccupation with "unconscious elements in personality, pre-eminence of drive, need, personality defense and sublimation in the organization and maintenance of behavior." He advances a new cognitive emphasis and identifies the school as the logical place for employing rational approaches to not only self-understanding, the teaching of dynamics of behavior, and the control of behavior but also "the explicit support of values" and "the maintaining of self records." By providing opportunities and incentives to achieve the "examined life," the school and its counselors can encourage the pupil to exercise rationality toward himself and others.

In Thorne's (1950) view "personality counseling" is a procedure in which the practitioner gathers an intricate series of diagnostic facts and applies a specific therapeutic technique, a model not unlike that of the physician who tracks down the pathology and administers a program of cure. While fully recognizing the forces of feeling, Thorne stresses such techniques as "maximizing intellectual resources" and "methods for intellectual reorientation." He cautions the counselor about his client's emotional attachments to him which may lead to unhealthy attitudes. The vast system of classification in this highly rational approach certainly appears to take into account many important emotional factors in the client's functioning. However, one gets the impression that in this method the counselor's preoccupation with his role of the knowing, directing, probing agent can easily result in an unfortunate de-emphasis of the live relationship between counselor and student.

No one doubts that there are many wise golden rules of behavior which have come down through the ages, not to speak of the dozens of current best sellers on how to lead a successful life. Nor do we overlook the possibility that many problems are simple or transitory. Parents often have to give direct advice where there are problems of immaturity or where expediency demands immediate answers. Peers may sometimes give excellent advice where they happen to recognize problems which they themselves have successfully solved. Counselors sometimes have to use "emergency powers" to provide immediate solutions. But we maintain that there are large areas of a person's life which remain untouched by advice giving and injunctions. What is generally required, particularly in our emotionally troubled and violent era, is to reach young people through sincere, real, and feeling relationships rather than through platitudinous "commonsense" advice giving which is too little, too late, and too often.

By seeking a purpose and a technique which could help all students rather than just those with specified problems, Berdie (1949) emphasizes the educational function of counseling. Not denying the importance of relationships or other useful tools of the sophisticated counselor, he devotes the bulk of his statement to stressing the sharing and clarification of ideas with the counselee. He should function "as a rational and feeling adult ready to enter into a constructive social-personal relationship with the student" rather than as an impersonal authority dealing only with the psychological conflict. With this statement he aligns himself with Williamson and other staff members of the University of Minnesota. His services for all students include an objective discussion of political, religious, and sexual beliefs, as well as personal goals, in an atmosphere of concern and sharing.

If content is stressed as an ingredient in counseling, making it an integral and working part of the counseling relationship is a more difficult task. A compelling argument for the "diagnostic interview" is made by Sachs (1966). Here the student goes through an open-ended period of questioning to provide the educator and counselor with information about and insight into the student and his world. Sachs states that "it is the integration of these aspects — the ability to feel at one with the student in the discussion and yet to be able to understand intellectually the underlying implication of his statements without judging or moralizing — that is at the heart of the ability to conduct the diagnostic interview."

Content-oriented counselors are neither primitive nor naive in their particular stressing of the powers of informing, suggesting, diagnosing, supporting, and persuading. They believe in trying to reach the most people in the least threatening way. Words and thoughts influence feelings and actions often enough to practice this approach with students relatively free of personal problems. In such cases teaching content suffices to promote change, since the interaction between counselor and student is relatively conflict free.

In a counseling session with a twelve-year old, Tammi complained that the science teacher was not consistent enough in his everyday moods and behavior. This inconsistency made her feel that the teacher was not preparing himself for his day's work adequately. Tammi resented this "unfairness" and was unable to concentrate in that class. The counselor chose to bring in content, specifically designing this intervention in keeping with the client's previous receptivity to rational, commonsense approaches. The counselor had also sensed Tammi's readiness to learn about the adult world from another adult. With this information in view, the counselor had a thirty-minute discussion about what could be unbalancing a teacher's day. This information gave the pupil facts about a working adult's day, making the parallel with the challenges and changes in the daily life of a youngster and parent. In this case, simply examining the content of her perception from another angle enabled the pupil to correct her distortions and the impatience which had contributed to her preoccupations and daydreaming.

The theme-centered interactional approach, which recognizes the reality of content, includes essential features of the cognitive school of thought. Content is valued as important. The counselee lacks knowledge. He needs to improve his effectiveness in living and in living-learning. Therefore choosing the theme of importance is one of the counselor's prominent tasks. The theme — content matter — is seen as the central issue of discussion between the counselor and his student or student group.

The process of teaching-learning depends primarily on intrapsychic and communicative factors in the counselor and intrapsychic and integrative elements in the counselee. But if these processes between teacher and learner are not flowing freely, the content which the counselor wishes to convey remains as remote from the counselee as the content of a book full of wisdom gathering dust on its shelf.

Accent on Process: Interpersonal and Intrapsychic

Like Moliere's surprised "Amateur Gentleman" who did not know he was speaking "prose," the counselor may not fully realize that he is using *process* when, for example, he maintains different goals and expectations for the beginning, middle, and ending phases of the counseling series. Certainly the counselee cannot be aware of "process" when anxiety or covert conflict makes him defensive. There are other interpersonal processes affecting communication and behavior which can be identified. The awareness, definition, and utilization of all of these processes make it possible for the counselor to perform on a professional level.

Rogers' client-centered philosophy is the outstanding example of how process can become the substance of effective counseling. Entering the scene in the 1940's, impressed with Rankian and relationship therapy as well as by Maslow, Lecky, Snygg and Combs, and others. Rogers gave personal counseling a therapeutic orientation. In effect, he opened the shutters of content to admit the light of process. His writings stressed the interpersonal as the "core of guidance."

The following six conditions necessary for personality change established by Rogers (1957) can readily be translated into group counseling terms:

1. Two persons are in psychological contact;
2. . . . the client is in a state of incongruence, being vulnerable or anxious;
3. . . . the therapist is congruent or integrated in the relationship.
4. 5. 6. the therapist experiences conditional positive regard . . . and an empathy . . . and endeavors to communicate this experience to the client . . .

Basing his theories of counseling and psychotherapy on "self-theory," Rogers stated that the key to change in the individual was to bring together into the self-structure an awareness of what others feel toward him and his own real feelings and experiences. This conscious combination makes possible the client's beginning to think, feel, and act in an integrated way.

The client's emotional reaching for and finding meaning in his own experienced world, essential for Rogers, is also the primary focus in the theory and practice of existential counseling. A major difference between the two viewpoints as discussed by Johnson (1967) is that Rogers stresses a deterministic drive of the organism toward health, while the existentialists view self-actualization more as volitional.

The existential philosophy asks questions about life which many counselors face in their everyday practice. Can we get to understand the other person through a discussion about things from the past or through a real-life, here-and-now existential encounter? Do we know a person better from reports of his obscure inner experiences or from the observable phenomenal world? Is a counseling relationship to be limited to sharing the social world while neglecting the deeply personal universe and private meanings of the counselee?

Strickland (1966) proposes answers to these questions. Through several processes, the existential counseling relationship ultimately aims at the client's freedom to make choices. These processes follow:

1. Permit the client to teach the counselor;
2. Understand the client's statements from his own frame of reference;
3. Employ any technique which will enable the client to find the truth from within;
4. Use objective knowledge sparingly because it may obstruct the self-knowledge of the client;
5. Let the client himself find the truth;
6. Encourage the client "in articulating all areas of his existence" which in turn may be defined as "a recurring, temporary, becoming phenomenon that represents the articulation of everything the individual is, has been, or strives to be with his own contemporary reality."

An existential encounter can fall short of the client's achieving specific goals or facing elusive problems. The concept of the client's "quest" formulated by Dole (1967) obliges the counselor to perform an immediate identification, clarification, and management of the purposes of the client. This action is seen as one of several processes which insure counseling success. Another has to do with maintaining the "purposive balance" where the counselor is helping, supporting, and understanding, while the counselee is planning, problem-solving, and self-actualizing. The "congruent counselor" is the one who permits the unfolding of these processes. The successful counselee is a "seeking, coping, thinking human being who requests aid voluntarily, (and) who may end the relationship when he wishes. . . . The congruent counselor realizes that he helps his client primarily because he is paid to do so. . . ." In this method we see reflected a hope that the complexities of counseling may be simplified by de-emphasizing the personal dynamics of the counselee and by focusing on his purposes. One may visualize this method as aiming at the meshing of a series of gears in the counseling process. However, in our view the complicated machinery of counseling cannot always be simplified by such a sophisticated approach through the "client's quest."

The term "psychoanalytic counselor" may sound discordant to those who still believe that the counselor's office is soundproofed from the clamor of the unconscious. As the training and experience of counselors and counselor educators expand, the theories of Freud, Jung, Adler, Rank, Sullivan, Horney, Fromm, and other "cultural" psychoanalysts find their place — in a fragmented way — in the work of counselors. Sullivan's (1954) description is a useful and brilliant example of the initial approach to the client, student, or patient. There is general acceptance of Adler's ideas about reaching children through their schools and families, his belief in the efficiency of short-term contacts, his stress on bringing out potentials, and achieving social integration. Each psychoanalytic theory is a fertile source for the counselor. Yet apparently there have been very few attempts by counselors to present a theory and technique of counseling which systematically blends concepts of any of the psychoanalytic schools.

An exception to this statement is Bordin's (1955) method of "psychological counseling," an outstanding if not unique example of a counselor's use of psychoanalytic process and the dynamics of human behavior. If without warning a psychoanalyst were removed from his office and assigned to a counselor's chair, he might function quite well as a counselor using Bordin's method. He might engage in similar processes, but not as deeply. Transference would be recognized, but not developed or interpreted. Resistance would be seen as an attempt to guard against infantile conflicts. Rather than trying to resolve the client's fixation to early psychosexual stages, the analyst would aim at increased insight into defenses by noting omissions, identifying contradictions, and reading physical movements. Important aspects of the client's inner world would be revealed to the searching spirit of the analyst-counselor and client. They would view past, present, and future with an emphasis on the present interaction.

Process in counseling is an abstraction which, while always present, is often unrecognized and unarticulated. It is variously thought of as the frame, rhythm, atmosphere, and ground of the counseling experience. Equal in importance to content, the process reveals not only the counselor's preferences of technique and style but also major aspects of how the client structures his world. Note the vicissitudes of process in the following incidents: a child is sent to the counselor with or without a frank, non-threatening explanation; the door to the counselor's office is open or closed; a counselor is of the same color and/or sex; interest tests are given before or after an exploratory session with the counselor; a high school student's parents are seen with or without the student's knowledge and consent.

A few examples of the appearance of process in counseling will serve to illustrate this key area. Early in the encounter the counselor receives signals about the client's personal processes: the puny fifth grader compensates by antagonizing; the stutterer controls by delayed or excessive verbalization; the withdrawn child retreats further through his drawing; the economically deprived student expresses his rage indiscriminately. The counselor's awareness of and empathy for such communications are part of his use of process both interpersonal and intrapsychic.

A "counseling plan" may well be one of the first processes employed. Whether implicit or explicit, a counselor draws up some sort of blueprint of his anticipations. This is by no means a push-button system used to impose control. Rather it is a tentative plan about the dynamics of the counseling situation geared to the counselee. What are his goals, and how well does he seem able to go forward? What are some of the student's characteristics which strengthen the counseling relationship, such as the ability to give and take, to be trusting, to be free of debilitating moods and conflicts, to be realistic yet daring about his immediate and longer term goals? The counseling plan cannot proceed very far if the counselor does not understand any of his own pervasive non-accepting or overattached feelings toward the student, Nor can there be much progress unless the counselor becomes aware of at least some of the client's realistic or projected perceptions of him.

The theme-centered interactional approach values process as an integral part of living. Process, therefore, is both means and goal.

Process is seen as creative progress through interaction. Process is change by openness and give and take with any other and, in group counseling, with the group. The theme-centered interactional method requests that each person in the group — group members (counselees) and group leader (counselor) — give to and take from the group what each individual desires to give and take during inter-action centering around a given theme. This give and take of the living-learning workshop in interaction is both model for and integral part of living-learning in society. The established group structure in which interaction takes place highlights and imparts the living-learning process — the dialectic of creative growth. Such growth in human existence includes the role of the elder and the role of the younger, exemplified in the roles of the counselor (group leader) and the participant (group member). However, as its members mature, the group accepts the responsibility for guarding the rules and the spirit which establish the structure as the foundation of fluid inter-action. These rules are geared toward awareness of the individual's autonomy, the group's interaction, and the penetration of the theme.

As the group progressively takes more responsibility for functioning within the given structure, the leader may at times relinquish the role of "chairman of the group" and become like an authentic group member, "chairman of himself." He then functions as the older person who is more experienced and often wiser than the younger counselees, a fact which in itself stimulates "growth" in his younger colleagues-in-living.

Focus on Human Development

One of the basic concerns of the counselor is the evaluation of the level or status of a student in comparison to others of his age as well as the assessment of variations and meanings of a given trend within the individual. With culturally deprived people, the counselor cannot use Gesell or other developmental norms as yardsticks with which to compare a child's optimism or extroversion at a given age. Instead, he must understand the level and quality of a student's intrapsychic *development* in the light of his own group norms as well as weighing environmental effects on the individual's past and present. The counselor, as much as any other professional in the school, sees his function as being strongly determined by the need to study and understand the student as a learning organism in the process of intellectual, physical, emotional, and social development.

Tiedemann (1965) proposes that guidance and counseling serve as liberating influences for the individual; their function is to guide and release the client's potential for growth. The student's "discontinuity" is what results from the gap between the student's ever developing self and the changing environment. While teaching creates "useful discontinuity" in terms of challenging, new, problem-solving situations, "guidance on the other hand, deals with the individualized reduction of the student's discontinuity."

Tiedemann advances an integrated approach based on various behavioral sciences to aid the individual in his "resolution of discontinuity."He illustrates with the college freshman orientation counselor. This person would represent to the student the college "system" which the student has just joined. By defining the new environment with particular emphasis on its differences from the student's past life, the counselor seeks to activate some of the student's developing adaptive mechanisms with the aim of helping the student master changed aspects of his environment; he helps him to progress toward "continuity."

Seeking to "broaden the base of guidance-personnel work," Zaccaria (1965) amalgamates the concepts of developmental tasks (Havinghurst), vocational-developmental tasks (Super), and psycho-social crises (Erikson) by formulating their common elements. He indicates how this formulation could serve subgoals of guidance by providing stepping stones to the main goal of guidance, which is developing a sense of identity. Zaccaria not only deals with the theoretical importance of the developmental concept but also indicates how in practice the counselor should work with the particular responses of the student to developmental tasks. The student's relationship to the task depends upon personality, culture, and intelligence factors. An individual varies according to the special *meaning* he assigns to the task, the attitude he assumes about *approaching* the task, and the *pattern of mastering* the task he follows.

These variations in the student's rate and manner of mastering developmental tasks not only provide counselors with useful reference points but also extend the common ground of teachers, counselors, and administrators. Even though enhancement of student development is nominally a major focus of school personnel, communication among staff members about means and goals tends to be restricted by differences in perspective and terminology. We feel that Zaccaria's work serves to bridge the gap. If developmental stages can be viewed in a broader and more integrated way — to include education, counseling, and psychoanalysis — the relationship between the pupil's personality and behavior may also be seen more consistently in classroom, counseling room, or principal's office.

Sanford (1962) calls attention to the importance of understanding the particular structure and stage of development of the college lower classman. While he logically directs his comments chiefly to the instructor who, in fact, spends most time with the student, Sanford's discussion of the student's personality provides the counselor with a valuable developmental emphasis. Sanford describes a high level of development as the expression of a greater degree of personality *differentiation* and *integration*.

The Freudian concepts of freeing impulses, enlightenment of conscience, and responsiveness and adaptability of the ego are employed by Sanford as a framework to judge the developmental level of the college freshman. Two conditions are required to promote growth to higher levels: the first is internal *readiness* or inner conditions; the second has to do with the promoting stimuli arising either from the person's body or his environment. Sanford realizes that to achieve this level of skill, the student must feel confident in expressing new responses, in "losing himself" undefensively, and in refusing premature imitation of adult behavior. Apprising himself of such developmental concepts, the college counselor can gain a more effective and rapid "feel" for the core, if not the seed, of the presenting problems.

The counselor is formally charged with the task of perceiving the student's progress in all its dimensions through accumulated records and in specialized interview and observational procedures. As the teacher shares an interest in all phases of intellectual and emotional growth, the counselor can help shoulder the burden of promoting this stream of development. When attuned to "growth," a counselor soon discerns that many requests for referral and consultation fall regularly into this very area.

On a recent examination for guidance counselors, there was the case of Jimmy, age eight, who was a gifted musician, a high academic achiever, but apparently infantile in social relationships. Jimmy was rapidly becoming more desperate in maintaining minimum self-esteem. Classwork, family life, and relationships with teacher and pupils were adversely affected. The candidates answering this question tended to overlook the possibilities for helping Jimmy to become interested in and to understand his developmental discrepancies. Rather they concentrated on direct efforts to reach the boy's rejecting mother and the possibility of sending Jimmy to another school offering better musical instruction.

Jimmy might be more quickly reached and helped first by reducing the elements of the problem into their developmental components and second by formulating a plan for counseling goals. The unevenness of development first suggests the need for an encounter with an adult who will work on building interpersonal competence — with emphasis upon Jimmy's acquiring greater empathy and autonomy. The child had a serious deficiency in the give and take of peer relationships which in turn contaminated his outlook on the classroom living situation. The counselor would moreover focus on Jimmy's flawed general judgment as well as his curtailed creativity in music, the very skill which could serve as a fulcrum for increased satisfaction and confidence. Any other example taken at random would also serve to confirm that if the counselor maintains his developmental orientation, he is in a position to fulfill the promise of his training and assignments. It is through the counselor, himself an organic part of the school, that the pupil can best experience the ebb and flow of his development within the ongoing process of school life.

The TCI leader has to meet the counselees wherever they are in the given here-and-now of their development. If the leader is unaware of the emotional and mental level of any group member, the member does not feel recognized and accepted for what he is at the present. The TCI leader recognizes the group as a source of cohesiveness and interaction, the best springboards for bringing out potentials of human development. During childhood and adolescent development, we see imbalances of the social, intellectual, and emotional. The TCI experience helps to balance these various aspects of growth through alternations of emphasis on the group, the theme, and the self.

Use of the Counselor's Self as Instrument

In the distant 1940's, when therapeutic activity by psychologist and counselor was considered avant garde (if not downright subversive!). I recall one of the early efforts of my supervisor to focus on personal feelings in the counselor-client relationship. In the middle of a case presentation he asked rather abruptly: "How do you like your client?" I was stunned by this innocent but deadly sounding question. Whatever feelings had been present initially with this client I had neatly subjugated in the service of interviewing, counseling, and testing. And if there had been some dislike for the client, a valiant effort at frankness and aplomb was needed to explain to the supervisor how I had handled these feelings. Fortunately such training drama became outdated as psychological counseling matured and neglected areas such as countertransference became more widely noticed in psychoanalytic practice. In social work it was recognized that a coalescing of the "diagnostic" school and the "functional" approach would be needed to provide the case-worker with more flexibility.

A few distinctions are needed before proceeding with this section on *counselor's self* as instrument. Countertransference, rarely mentioned as such by counselors, is defined as a *distorted* reaction by the counselor in terms of a particular unresolved problem of his past. Another definition of countertransference is the counselor's reaction to his distorting the view of his client, an induced reaction. In the first instance the counselor may identify too strongly with a student who reports academic pressure from a father because this same problem lies unresolved in the counselor's personal history. In the second instance a girl acting seductively might arouse in the female counselor a countertransference of fear because of the implications of homosexuality engendered by the student's transference. In this induced reaction, the counselor feels drawn to complying with the girl's wishes because of her own submissiveness.

Another aspect of the counselor's personal reaction refers to a shared openness in which, however, he must seek to avoid distortions about himself, the counselee, or the counseling relationship. This practice would exclude the imposition of troubled areas of his personality which might demand resolution at the expense of the client. A political discussion which includes too many personal reactions by the counselor borders on this problem. If undefensive, most things can be said by the counselor, provided that they increase honest communicativeness. A measured remark by the counselor about his fatigue or tension at the moment could serve cathartically to alleviate or remove a disturbing attitude. Experiments in encounter and other groups which foster symmetrical relationships have shown us that openness and candor add to the richness of the experience.

In the following pages are illustrations of counselors serving as stimulating, liberating, and refreshing influences. In our present tendency toward mass education, mass media, and ubiquitous computers, it is incumbent upon the counselor really to be himself and survive these person-leveling forces.

According to Arbuckle (1966) only by being "free" — that is, by fulfilling himself in his own actions, by permitting himself to "show through clearly" — can the counselor promote meaningful experience with his clients. Also the very struggle toward self-actualization must not be forgotten, for it is only when the counselor has achieved this process for himself and remembers it that he can guide his counselee through the same maze. With such free flow of being one's self, the counselor can function at a high level in establishing an empathic relationship within the client's frame of reference and in being "genuine and honest" with another human being.

In a similar vein Dreyfus (1967) believes that the most important force for change in counseling and therapy is the counselor's "genuineness and authenticity" as a person. Freedom in expression and the ability to be completely oneself may serve as models for the client who seeks authenticity as a person. Discarding gimmicks and techniques — even disregarding the dangers of countertransference — the counselor is free to provide a warm, accepting attitude, a true encounter, proof that feelings are not bad or dangerous. If alienation is one of the chief ills of the day, the counselor must provide the opposite for relief. In fact the author cares less about the educational and psychological training of the counselor in the academic sense than he does about emphasizing in training programs the increased self-awareness, sensitivity, and spontaneity of the trainee.

Shoben (1965) stops short of advising the counselor to be fully himself, suggesting that it is more realistic to be "his professional self." In this view it is not desirable or necessary for the counselor to expose his entire self (as a spouse or employer or friend might see him), since he can in the more rarified act of counseling provide an ego-ideal not encumbered by his neurotic tendencies. It almost appears that Shoben's counselor is encouraged to *mimic* "good parents" and to *bestow* love and understanding rather than to be this kind of person. The "nice" counselor seeking to gain rapport is suspect to Shoben, since this way of acting not only is too superficial but also may put the counselor "in the position of having appeared to promise far more than he is either willing to deliver, or that would be therapeutically appropriate."

In effect Shoben assumes a midpoint position between the uninvolved analyst and the deeply involved transactionalist. He suggests that it is easier for the counselor to act more ideally in the "unencumbered" counseling relationship than in other life encounters. There are many who would be skeptical of this "professional" approach to the student for the following reasons:

1. Would not a sensitive client become preconsciously aware of inconsistencies in the personality of such a counselor?
2. Would not such a counselor with interpersonal tension in many "real-life" situations experience some of the same unresolved problems with his client?
3. Would not such a counselor tend to slip into intellectual defenses and find all too many reasons to engage in expounding an excess of information — giving and conceptualizing which are not needed or sought after by the client?

The counselor cannot successfully encourage self-expression, exploration of one's intrinsic worth, and a free flowing relationship with the outer world if he himself is "culturally encapsulated." In these terms Wrenn (1965) correctly deals with what might be considered as the resistance of the counselor to change. If this basic impediment is not removed, the counselor will be unable to function adequately in his own relationship to the developing personalities of his clients. Instead of wrapping himself in the safety of the past, the counselor is given directions which would help him to respond fully to his students. Wrenn asks that the counselor not be taken by surprise when the accepted truth changes. What may have been considered the "right" age for "going steady" may well have been modified in the light of present cultural developments. The gap in the personal experience of the counselor is sometimes too broad to bridge when he relies heavily on his own past in relating to young people. Wrenn adds that to engage in any real empathic encounter, the counselor cannot approach the young person influenced by conflicting feelings and values from a world of the past. The counselor instead, may maintain his own beliefs but must persist in learning the mores of other cultures and subcultures. Further he should encourage students whose thinking is different from his. Without being self-righteous, the counselor can have faith in his ideals. Most important, he must believe in himself and others as partners in the process of becoming.

The counselor's use of himself as a tool should include more of an objective orientation, according to Knowles and Barr (1968). Referring to studies describing the effective and creative person, the authors pursue the hypothesis that objective, cognitive, structured, scientific traits are needed to balance the danger of counseling becoming a wishy-washy subjective discipline. To rescue the practice of counseling from becoming mired in a one-sided emphasis, they conclude that "counselors need exposure to subjective and objective learning experiences and people." However, while Knowles and Barr validly seek a counselor who combines both qualities, their alarm about pseudo-subjectivity seems to result from a misunderstanding. Their complaint about subjectivity may be explained by the difficulty inherent in training future counselors to develop the subjective attitudes needed for minimally effective counseling. The emphasis on objectivity which is claimed to be missing is, on the contrary, well documented in counselor education. We prefer to underline the blending required by the good humanist-scientist-counselor.

That this dual emphasis can be crystallized is illustrated by the work of Buchheimer and others (1965), designed to study "empathy." A highly subjective reaction, "empathy," was described as involving role prediction, role assumption, and confluence (or mutual transference), all of which were made measurable through a video tape of an actual counseling session.

This blend of the subjective and objective may be illustrated by counseling in a logical and rational style, an approach which may have the favorable effect of relieving the client of what he perceives to be an overly charged relationship. The student may find it easier to benefit in an atmosphere of more objective searching for changed attitudes and values. He may not have the problem of being over-intellectualized (requiring a loosening of this defense by emotional confrontation), but rather he may habitually proceed smoothly from the intellectual to the emotional. A high school sophomore once taught a counselor that the "subjective" attitude of sensing and noting the student's immediate non-verbal communications was unwanted and unhelpful. Heeding this advice, the counselor no longer hesitated to bring up topics about counseling and therapy, a practice which engaged the student fully in a meaningful relationship and which eliminated his tendency in the earlier sessions toward long, unproductive silences. It soon became apparent that these discourses were being used profitably — although cautiously — as part and parcel of a deeper emotional involvement.

In this section we have elucidated some of the factors which make the counselor a more sensitive instrument. To satisfy the artistic and scientific requirements of his job, he is virtually expected to turn himself inside out when necessary. He is asked to make good use of his various "selves." Love and understanding alone for the client will not work unless the counselor is fully tuned in to his own perceptions and reactions in a given session. But the counselor needs to be more than warm, empathic, committed, and possessed of all the familiar assets and skills; nor can we add up a list of qualities and predict that they will work in a given situation. Rather the structure or configuration of the counselor's personality must provide the kind of synthesis which can be harnessed to the counseling. In this way the counselor who may be lacking in degrees of warmth, empathy, commitment, or other skills can still reach the counselee effectively through a unique blend of qualities consisting of past experience, knowledge of counseling and himself, and maximum employment of his own personality skills.

In the following excerpt from a graduate student's report, one may observe a number of interfering attitudes which normally might be expected to interfere with counseling effectiveness. Despite this fact the supervisor of the case recognized positive movement.

> "Although she was accepting of my role I was made to feel uncomfortable because I could only counsel how to help her adjust to a new situation, while what I felt she really wanted was to have the situation changed . . . My basic respect for C. as a socially mature, respecting, individual capable of self-dignity, flagged during her periods of long, almost endless whining complaint . . . In the final interview, C. seemed so hopeful and confident that she had been helped and was ready to proceed on her own that I was not able to suggest to her that we needed to continue our sessions . . . I could not bear to cast the slightest shadow

on her hopeful attitude . . .

Ruth C. Cohn's theme-centered interactional method, developed from her countertransference workshop, was designed to deal with and to resolve acute countertransference situations in the psychoanalyst's practice. As a participant leader her emphasis has been on the acceptance of "whatever is" as preferable to the demand of "what should be." If the leader accepts whatever disturbs his or other participants' functioning as a matter of course, he avoids the kind of moralism which promotes denial and lying. The spirit of the theme-centered interactional workshop promotes the acceptance of weakness in both counselor and counselee together with their wish to function better. Progress can then be made with minimal pain (the pain resulting from the masochistic banging of one's head against the wall of guilt) and optimal success. As the leader need not hide his fallibility behind the cloak of being the kind or perfect parent or the all-knowing teacher and wise guru, he can use all his energy — usually wasted on hiding — in the service of creativity. The counselor's productive self-use stimulates the counselees to shed some of their own unnecessary and destructive self-deceiving and lying equipment and to search for their personal truth.

Efforts at Combining and Integrating

The following section on *combining and integrating* presents a wide scatter of methods ranging from behavioral counseling (or learning theory approaches to counseling) to a system influenced by group dynamics. What we attempt to illustrate are examples of a multiple focus, underlining a need for synthesis in counseling. Here the counselor is seen as adopting eclecticism or pragmatism to weave together a variety of elements which he uses adaptively according to the particular client or situation. This statement is not to imply that the previous writers neglect flexibility in their work.

One of the major currents in counseling theory today is eclectic counseling which essays the synthesis or *integration* of "client-centered" and "clinical" approaches. Boy and Pine (1968) report on the dialogue between Carl R. Rogers and Edmund G. Williamson during which the two divergent points of view were compared with respect to values, place of diagnosis, voluntary and involuntary counseling, use of tests, self-determination and counselor responsibility, information collecting, and goals. The eclectic chooses to be more directive or more client-centered, depending upon his personality and the requirements of the situation. He modulates the emphasis from a "clinical," guiding, evaluating orientation to a relationship, "client-centered" spirit, depending upon the presenting problem, the client, or even the particular stage of counseling.

Confronted with the burgeoning array of technical variations, requirements on the job, and research findings in counseling, the eclectic manages to keep his balance on the moving platform of an evolving profession. He understands that he has ingrained values of his own, yet he aims at having his counselee explore a choice of values with as little interference as possible. He realizes that a "diagnosis" must sometimes be delivered to referring sources, if not to the student himself, but at the same time he avoids having this process jar the counseling relationship. He prefers a voluntary client but is amenable to taking an unmotivated student by the hand and leading him to the counselor's office. He comprehends the advantages of testing and information collecting in terms of time saving and greater objectivity but will not jeopardize the counseling relationship by juxtaposing tests and information gathering. While he values the goal of a more basic reorientation of personality and an emotional release of forces for growth, he still finds it useful to deal intellectually with the client in a dialogue about problems and problem solving. If the counselor wants to do things which will help alleviate symptoms and problems and which will serve to eliminate disorganizing attitudes and unrealistic goals, such eclecticism would seem justified.

Fullmer and Bernard (1964) view the various theoretical issues on a continuum, advising the counselor to mix his own brew, so long as he understands the what, why, and how of his decision. Whichever system he adopts, the counselor will base his practice on some variation of these authors' eclectic dichotomies or contrasts:

Authoritarianism or permissiveness
Persuasion or advice
Intellectual interpretation or change wrought by emotion
Catharsis or sharing
External or internal frame of reference
Open or closed system of counseling
Immediate problem solving or achieving growth and development

Immediate or long-term goals
Knowing or being
The individual as a problem or the situation as a problem
Here-and-now or historical approach
Folklore and myth or validations of assumptions and
  research
Verbal insight or behavior and attitude changes as evidence
  of progress
Individual traits and facts or the total person as a structure
  and process.

Our own view of an eclectic approach is illustrated here:

Alfred, a college student, age 18, referred himself to the counseling service a few months into the semester following his return from a year's leave of absence. He was obese, sloppy, and seal-like, with short arms and ambling gait. He had a soft-pleasing look, but his words were emitted explosively and voraciously. He was clearly aware of multiple problems: apprehension and uneasiness with everyone; difficulty with handwriting and foreign language; long history of being rejected and teased by peers; conflict with a father who had a "different orientation"; overprotection by mother "who would calm me down."

The counselor decided to use a structured, supportive, and briefer approach, aimed at encouraging him to remain at the college. A casual, understanding friendliness by the counselor was indicated, since anything "closer" would have precipitated Alfred's view of the counselor as an indulgent, weakening influence.

In the course of the five sessions, Alfred formulated his problem with increasing insight and in transactional terms: "If I do a lot for somebody and be humble, this person will like me and listen to me and consider me to be intellectually gifted." The counselor showed that humbleness was not rewarded and that Alfred was accepted without having to demonstrate high levels of accomplishment with college index, girl friends, and parents. All along, the counselor believed that Alfred would do better to remain in school. This belief might be described as a "tentative goal" based on evidence developed during the counseling. No doubt this was sensed by Alfred as a "good expectation," uncontaminated by overprotection, ambivalence or coercion. The counselor encouraged Alfred to talk about his experiences in "sticking it out" during difficult periods of his life. Alfred decided to remain in school.

A follow-up two years later indicated in the college records that Alfred was still in attendance, majoring in urban sociology, and planning to do research in this area. He did not return for further counseling.

Hummel's (1965) effort to integrate psychological theory and counseling method is stated as "ego-counseling." He uses an ego concept which depicts an actively expanding organism organizing his own reality. Borrowing from the concept of "sector," (coined by Felix Deutch in the practice of short-term psychotherapy), Hummel explains that in ego-counseling "the counselor influences the counseling deliberations as early as his assessment of a counselee warrants so that a gradual focus is made . . . on some role or situation . . . determined by the setting . . . reason for referral . . . or/and idiosyncratic features of the counselee's life situation."

While trying to bridge the two psychological worlds of behaviorism and phenomenology, Wrenn (1965) first stressed their differences, if not their irreconcilability. He thought that the behaviorist's emphasis on means is a way of engineering human beings at odds with the humanist-counselor emphases upon the nature and meaning of the goals. Yet Wrenn believed that at our present stage of theory construction, no doors should be closed. He spanned the two apparently disparate approaches as follows:

"The first (self-psychology) contributes to the examination of meaningful ends or purposes of a counseling relationship . . . while the second (behaviorism) can contribute a meaningful method for producing desired change in behavior or attitudes. The human being is more than a reacting organism, he is an integrating organism . . . How he perceives himself and others is a significant factor in how he responds to stimuli and situations . . . Counseling involves, or perhaps is, a learning process but the content material of the learning is the learner, not something exterior to him. And this adds to the learning process an element of individual meanings of self and world."

Turning now to *learning theory approaches* to counseling, we find a rather broad integrative emphasis. Any effort involved in human change includes some form of learning; learning theories and application are many and diverse.

The essence according to "behavioral counselors" is the learning process and the use of behavioral science method (such as experimental research procedures) to advance the client's ability to resolve his difficulties. The counselor accomplishes this advancement by ascertaining the goals and behavior of the client and then planning an appropriate technique of learning. According to McDaniel (1966), instead of asking what the theory indicates about counseling for this client, the behavioral counselor asks "what procedures seem most likely to help this client learn to engage in the kind of activities that will produce the satisfaction he wants." Typically, attention is paid to a highly specific problem or situation and to an appropriate application of learning theory to alleviate the problem.

Behavior changes according to Krumboltz (1966) are classified into three categories of goals each calling for a different approach by the counselor:

1. *Altering maladaptive behavior.* Here the problem and goal have to be stated explicitly by client and counselor as encompassing a desire for a specific change of behavior. If, for example, the student wants to do something about his shyness in class, the counselor proceeds by helping him analyze the situation which calls forth the shyness followed by discussions of more constructive and satisfying ways of reacting to the stimulus.
2. *Learning the decision-making process.* The goal is to have the counselee learn to use a series of problem-solving steps beginning with how to gather feasible alternatives and concluding with how to formulate a tentative plan of action subject to new developments. The most frequent opportunity is where the student asks for ready answers about vocational plans. Here the counselor can provide an experience in the use of information about interest and skills to teach the techniques of "narrowing the choices."
3. *Preventing problems.* The goal is to instruct and enlighten the counselee, agency, and institution about the logically sound or unwise steps that may accompany

a person's actions and decisions. If, for example, the teaching methods for a given child may be demonstrated as inappropriate, this faulty procedure might be avoided.

Behavioral counselors have developed four general approaches to the development of counseling techniques which are classified by Krumboltz into the following:

1. *Operant learning.* The timing of reinforcement is useful in producing the kind of behavior desired by the client. Thus an A grade and other forms of approval encourage and reinforce behavior.
2. *Imitative learning.* The client is shown models of behavior to emulate.
3. *Cognitive learning.* The client needs to know, understand, and utilize crucial information. Role playing is cited as a useful technique in this area.
4. *Emotional learning.* By pairing an unpleasant reaction with a pleasant and relaxed feeling, the client is gradually "inoculated against stress." This approach is derived from the clinical conditioning paradigm used by Solpe, Lazarus, and others.

While a variety of learning theories and concepts may easily be spelled out, the task of applying them to counseling is another matter. In case studies reported by behavior therapists and counselors and cited by Breger and McGaugh (1967), a wide variety of activities went on during a session — for example, discussions, explanations, and unearthing memories — making it difficult to ascribe any changes to specific learning techniques. To overcome this theoretical problem and to introduce a single technique, Breger and McGaugh suggest treating neurotic behavior by exposing the person to an individual or group situation where in order to be understood, he must "develop a new 'language,' a new set of central strategies." Hence he is forced into developing more insight into past fixations by way of searching for a language others will understand.

In a discussion of learning theory and counseling, a distinction must be made between two separate but related approaches. The discussion above referred to *the utilization of models of learning theory for counseling.* This method is differentiated from the approach of Alexander (1946), Shoben (1965), and others who do not seek to eliminate or radically modify the existing forms of counseling and therapy. Rather they wish to have us understand the learning principles which are operating in a variety of therapeutic methods. Thus learning about oneself and finding the freedom to change are enhanced when, as in practically every method, the therapist is patient and provides favorable learning conditions, free of censure. Whether learning theory is used to build new models in counseling or whether we identify the learning principles inherent in existing models, the two approaches share the basic task of reducing the client's anxiety and of freeing his communications.

The theme-centered interactional theory and practice, having been receptive to various group work influences, is holistic and interpersonal, combining and integrating a variety of existing trends and emphases. People are seen as interrelated psychobiological units. Every single event or multiple experience derived from external or internal sources (the environment or the somato-psychic self) changes the totality of the human being and his interrelatedness with his material and human environment.

II

Counseling
and
Guidance
Groups

The identification of essential and unique features in counseling enables the group counselor to perceive the group experience multi-dimensionally. The five elements of Chapter I find fertile ground in the group modality. Content, process, human development, the counselor's self, efforts at combining and integrating — all are valuable constructs used in varying proportions by the group leader according to his goals for the group, both its members and himself. We offer now some basic definitions and descriptions of group guidance and group counseling practices which were built up on the foundation of these five elements.

Group Guidance Procedures

Group Guidance is generally defined as a method in which cognitive material of an academic and non-academic nature is the content of an informal, cooperative, interactive classroom meeting. Emphasis is also placed on the group's reaching decisions, studying its own working, and learning how to satisfy the needs of its members. Group guidance is oriented toward the developmental needs of an individual, personally, socially, and intellectually. The skills needed in guidance combine those of a sensitive, intuitive teacher and group dynamicist. There are rich examples of the use of group dynamics in guidance, as described by Glanz (1962), Bennett (1963), and Lifton (1967).

The group guidance worker engages chiefly in a task-oriented approach. He employs many of the learning techniques of the teacher. An important difference is that generally the teacher is not in a position to be as informal, permissive, and focused on the self of the student. Group techniques inherent in group guidance are described by Bennett (1963) as based on group dynamics research. Among the procedures in use are appropriate leadership, democratic atmosphere, cohesiveness of the group, sociometric techniques, techniques of listening, types of contributions to discussion, joint problem-solving techniques, role playing, case-method discussion, and self-appraisal techniques. Obviously group guidance as a philosophy and methodology has been receptive to group dynamics.

The common purpose of group guidance (and group dynamic classroom groups) is to lubricate the wheels of learning interaction by opening up emotional and sensory doors for ingesting new ideas. This emphasis is seen as a move to a more favorable context from the one where the teacher manipulates facts, concepts, and charts like a chess player: now the teacher and students become explorers who begin to enter into whatever they are discovering. Through interaction not only do we derive the profound and largely untapped benefits of peer teaching-learning, but also the group process makes the students' apperceptive mass more available for receiving the newly relevant information.

Group process in educational groups has not flowered because of the overbalanced emphasis on knowledge and the need to present an ever increasing volume of facts, reflecting the growth of available findings in our generation. The group-oriented teacher and group guidance worker seek to revive the benefits of group process which have become lodged in the special areas of group therapy, inspirational groups, and various kinds of clubs and social organizations. To do so is to bring back to education a whole range of elements that can be useful; this effort is akin to bringing back the life-giving circulation of blood from the limbs into the body of pedagogy. Some direct applications of TCI to teaching-learning may be found in Chapter XI.

In the following tables we summarize the basic structural elements of group guidance and classroom groups. As with succeeding tables, we begin with simple working definitions and theoretical bases and assumptions. We then outline sources of referral, specific aims and benefits, and usual duration and composition of the groups described. Then we focus on the actual procedures, including typical content, and on the nature and sequence of the sessions. This brings us to the group leader and his points of reference followed by the member and his functions and reactions, including degrees of cooperation and reality testing. Finally we describe the uniqueness of the particular group experience.

Basic Group Counseling

Group Counseling has evolved by absorbing a wide range of useful theory and practice, resulting in many models. Yet it is agreed that group counseling "is a dynamic interpersonal process through which individuals within the normal range of adjustment work within a peer group . . . exploring problems and feelings . . . so that they are better able to deal with developmental problems (Cohn, B., p.355). In discussing their work with group counselors, we often hear of ingenious adaptations from other fields or of insights from research findings in counseling and psychotherapy.

In organizing personal counseling groups, the counselor seeks referrals of students with a wide range of intellectual, social, and emotional difficulties. Typically his aims are "educative" in the sense described by Wolberg (1967): "deliberate efforts at readjustment, goal modification, and the living up to existing creative potentialities, with or without insight of unconscious conflicts." This kind of group also contributes to developing greater skill, satisfaction, and security in the give and take of interpersonal relationships.

TABLE 1
Group Guidance

1. *Definition*	Stress on cognitive, informational element of a non-academic nature using informal, liberating, self-directing discussions and techniques which throw some light on the personality of the group member.
2. *Theoretical Basis*	Within this group, the student can help and be helped in significant content areas of his life. At a point between education and counseling, guidance uses content and process to reach students personally, yet non-threateningly.
3. *Referral*	Either voluntary or compulsory attendance.
4. *Aims — Benefits*	To provide greater participation, communication, and cooperation in the process of living education.
5. *Duration and Composition*	Class size, ranging from one session to an entire semester or year.
6. *Ground Rules*	To bring oneself into the discussion freely and responsibly; to discover the obstacles to participation and make efforts to share them or overcome them.
7. *Content*	Educational, social, vocational, and personal issues related to human development.

8. *Special Nature of Experience* — Provides a less formal outlet for frank and personal reactions on a wide scale often unavailable in a classroom.

9. *Stages — Sequences* — Follows more or less the sequence of a curriculum, covering phases of the topics selected.

10. *Leader* — On the model of a "master teacher": is knowledgeable about children's developmental concerns, can teach and demonstrate interestingly and can make "positive and sensitive" contact with participants.

11. *Member* — Requires a shift from the usual classroom learning to a more attitudinally and expressively centered discussion.

12. *Motivation — Resistance* — Resistance can be brought on by dullness of leader, participants or content. Motivation depends on the lively quality of the discussion by involved participants.

13. *Transferences — Realities* — As in a classroom, transferences are not dealt with directly and are subject to continuous consensual validation by the frequency of interaction.

14. *Uniqueness* — By anticipating concerns in the developmental process and by meeting those needs, group guidance provides meaningful learning experiences which can facilitate understanding and decision making and develop positive regard for self and others (Gazda and Folds).[1]

[1]Gazda, G.M. and Folds, J.H., Group Guidance: A Critical Incidents Approach, Parkinson Division, Follett Educational Corporation, 1968.

TABLE 2

Classroom Groups

1. *Definition*	A formal work group using knowledge of group organization and structure to enhance classroom learning.
2. *Theoretical Basis*	The social context provides for fuller learning by experiencing.
3. *Referral*	Pupils are assigned involuntarily.
4. *Aims — Benefits*	Group forces such as group norms, group goals, and leadership directed to create a climate of learning.
5. *Duration and Composition*	From ten to fifty students of approximately the same age but with a wide range of intellectual, social, and physical characteristics; usually for one semester or one year.
6. *Ground Rules*	(Vary widely) Attend lectures, discussions, and activities; cooperate with teacher and others; achieve as much learning as possible for oneself, while establishing sharing and tolerant relationships with classmates.
7. *Content*	Subject-matter learning, social learning.
8. *Special Nature of Experience*	Opportunity for the student to study the effects of his behavior as a worker-learner on the group, and vice-versa, and to find ways of en-

hancing his learning and achieving as a group member.

9. *Stages — Sequences*

Beginning as individuals, through interaction pupils become cohesive, co-operative, sharing, productive, and, finally, skilled in removing barriers and generating energy for learning.

10. *Leader*

May be teacher-centered or group-centered, directive or non-directive. Needs understanding and skills of interaction with students; needs to be clear about subject orientation or social behavior orientation. Integration of (1) attention to individual's development, (2) group development and organization, (3) curriculum.

11. *Member*

Full use of his own resources in preparing for and participating in class. Has to relate appropriately at chosen moments to maximize the learning possibilities offered by teacher and peers.

12. *Motivation — Resistance*

Both factors can become extremely high depending on the successful use of group process.

13. *Transferences — Realities*

Continuous, long-term interaction in a variety of parameters provides reality testing and feed-back which make interactions subject to continu-ous consensual validation.

14. *Uniqueness*

The holistic nature of the task of classroom group dynamics, spanning the individual, the group, the task, and the enveloping environment.

A closed group — starting and stopping as a unit — would seem to be the most natural and workable arrangement in relatively short-term school groups. Counselors have found it easier to work with a group sharing the same problem area, a practice which is consistent with the recommendations of "short-term" group therapists (Wolf). Concern for the use or abuse of drugs, problems of giving and taking with the opposite sex, conflicts over studying and learning — all are areas which would attract groups with an important, cohesive starting point. Yet the range of personality differences within each of the groups would provide the necessary balance, stimulation, and deviation to promote a forward, mutually contributing movement. This practice is clearly supported by Boy and Pine (1968), who say that "within a school there are natural clusters of students who have sought out each other's company because of the comfort they feel in the association with certain types of peers. This . . . natural homogeneity . . . (and) ease of communication enhance the process of group counseling."

Certain processes commonly employed in personal group counseling stand out as perhaps specific to this procedure. The group counselor, in the relatively brief time he has, is engaged in uncovering, exploring, and alleviating the problem of maladjustive behavior with each of the voluntary participants through gradual confrontations and with the active participation of the other group members as auxiliary counselors. The behavior of the individual (or of the *group* where the orientation is "group centered") is frequently studied as an echo of the past. But at all times the living, ongoing, laboratory aspect of the experience is used to encourage new "realistic," "authentic," and "satisfying" experiments in decision making and self-expression. The leader's role is to encourage interaction and identification, at the same time upholding the integrity of each person and his right to develop his own potentiality. The leader aims at subordinating but not submerging himself, functioning in Froehlich's phrase "from within the group."

The place and advisability of intensive or personal counseling (and psychotherapy) in society and, more specifically, in the educational framework are open to controversy. The range of comment extends from "does psychotherapy work?" to "let's bring more of the benefits of psychology and psychiatry to overburdened and antiquated institutions." The fact is today that therapeutic counseling approaches are sorely needed as resources in our schools and other settings at least until such time as these institutions can more effectively srve the individuals for whose good they were created.

The following chart presents a model of basic group counseling. Charts on family counseling and activity and play groups may be seen in Chapter IV. These are all clearly influenced by the medical model. The doctor diagnoses and then attempts to treat the symptoms or heal the patient. He is the expert in the causation and dynamics of inner and outer stress on the functioning human being. In this sense the patient is not unlike the client, student, or parent who comes for alleviation of his pain in living. Not immediately recognizing the source or meaning of this pain, the client is helped to gain such insight or to strengthen existing weakness, to correct deficiencies, to overcome developmental blocks, to alleviate dissatisfactions in living, and to develop improved interactional patterns — all through the combined efforts of others in a group.

The school counselor who wants to go beyond academic advisement or guidance has been drawn to the therapeutic model because it is one of the few available to him and because of the understandable demands made upon him to bring those with deviated or disruptive behavior back into the fold of education. Yet most counselors in their therapeutic work are not satisfied to be "school doctors." Their eyes are fixed on the broader educational goals of the whole person, genuine dialogue (in Buber's meaning), and the stimulation of the learner's powers by the demands of social situations (in Dewey's sense).

Multidimensional Guidance and Counseling in Groups

Several examples of a versatile and integrative use of guidance and counseling have appeared. We review them here and make some comparisons with the TCI approach.

"Multiple counseling" as described by Driver (1962) represents an attempt to tie group discussion and group dynamics to a counseling setting. The author states that this method does not follow psychoanalysis but rather social psychology and psychiatry, utilizing "human relationships as a learning instrument . . . growth away from egocentricity toward altruism . . . stress on interpersonal relationships rather than inner conflict . . ." Also in this method the author stresses discussions and learning of facts about personal and social adjustment and "conjunctive individual counseling" in which the group leader discusses in an individual session what he has learned about the client during the group session. To differentiate the method further, Driver lists the following differences with group therapy:

1. Group members are not forced into self-revelation;
2. "Topic" approach is introduced by the leader;
3. Enjoyment of sessions is considered important;
4. Leader is not limited to non-directive methods.

While one may question whether points (1) and (4) represent group therapy accurately, her method is an example of an imaginative approach to group counseling, loosely but colorfully woven of many threads. Many of these threads are the same as those in theme-centered interactional workshops, leading to the conclusion that multiple counseling represents an early model or precursor of the method introduced in this book. The chief differences between the two methods may be described in four ways:

(1) *Integration and Blending.* While multiple counseling includes elements of group discussion, group dynamics, counseling, mental hygiene, and psychiatry, it does not quite establish a system in which these elements are integrated and coordinated into a specific method. Rather a series of techniques are strung out and tend to be utilized discretely. The following are used: discussion, interaction, group counseling, individual counseling, mental hygiene, psychology of differences, topic centeredness and problem centeredness. Multiple counseling would appear to be a rich collection of sub-methods rather than a unified one.

(2) *Depth of Focus on Individual.* Multiple counseling tends to avoid dealing directly with the individual's inner thoughts and feelings during the group session but rather relegates this study to a "conjunctive" individual session or "dissolves" conflicts through interaction and group dynamics.

(3) *Use of Theme.* The multiple counseling theme is not employed as the persistent rallying point from which excursions are made into past and future individual and group experience. In the theme-centered interactional approach there is more emphasis on cognition and the

content of the topics under discussion.

(4) *Problem Orientation.* One of the unique features of multiple counseling described by Froehlich and reported by Bennett (1963) is use of the "common problem." In the theme-centered interactional method the announced theme has a striving, compelling, and timely quality, but it is not expressed in terms of "a problem." However, in TCI counseling (Chapter XII) problems are in focus.

Lifton (1967) takes an important integrative step in group counseling. Cutting across the lines of education, guidance, counseling, and psychotherapy, he lists common denominators which include the following features of a group: people need security before they are able to expose themselves; topics pull a group together, and as there are digressions, each new topic can be used profitably; a successful group provides a feeling of acceptance for the members; a group is valuable for its reality-testing function; the importance of the individual's behavior and differences and his full participation are significant areas of focus; recognition of the influence of the past on current perceptions may be discussed.

By espousing the stepping down of the leader from his role, Lifton aims at preventing the leader from using the group "for his own needs" and at providing the members with the helpful challenge of dealing with an authority at an equal level. This recommendation leans toward the group dynamics model where there is more of a preoccupation with leadership roles. At the same time, Lifton seems to be identified with the therapy model in his concern for examining problems, solving problems, and the healing effects of groups.

Reviewing the main sample protocol of the book (Lifton, pp.67-109), we find a predominant number of the author's running comments devoted to group process: orientation, organization, interaction, and evolution. What Lifton claims to be an *integration of therapeutic techniques* appears to be rather the *therapeutic by-products* of an essentially group dynamics procedure. Direct therapy with the individual was more avoided than faced. Rather *certain* therapeutic effects may have been *facilitated* indirectly for *some* individuals by group processes. Let us examine this issue in the light of the sensitive *"A Dairy of the Complete Life of a Group,"* written by a group member (Lifton, pp.268-270). In "Log 21," one of the members had apparently asked for help with a personal problem. In re-

TABLE 3
Basic Group Counseling

1. Definition

Support, re-education, readjustment, or symptom relief to be achieved through counselor and group members. Variations include behavioral, analytically oriented, and client-centered counseling.

2. Theoretical Basis

Therapeutic relationship can benefit and influence. Identifications, multiple transferences, and cohesiveness are important constructs.

3. Referral

Wide range of difficulties: intellectual, social, emotional. Special variations such as emergency counseling where members of a group are under acute stress.

4. Aims — Benefits

Predominantly re-educative: "Deliberate efforts at readjustment, goal modification and the living up to existing creative potentialities with or without insight into conscious conflicts" (Wolberg). Additional aims related to developing greater skill, satisfaction, and security in the give and take of interpersonal relationships.

5. Duration and Composition

Four to ten students. Five to fifty sessions of one to one and a half hours each. Continuous (people in and out) or closed (all starting and stopping together). Homogenous or heterogeneous.

6. Ground Rules

Speak as freely as possible while respecting rights of others. No physical acting out.

7. *Content*
History, current environmental problems, intra-group reactions with focusing by counselor on personal-social adjustment, defense mechanisms, conflicts, growing up, and school learning.

8. *Special Nature of Experience*
Therapeutic insights, emotional release, increased awareness of self; relief from loneliness, tension, isolation.

9. *Stages — Sequences*
Initial (reconnaissance, rapport), middle (working through), and ending phases (separation, evaluation).

10. *Leader*
Various personality styles: authoritarian-permissive; individual-centered or group-centered.

11. *Member*
Willingness to change. Becoming a useful, productive member by serving oneself and the group through honest, open, committed, and involved participation.

12. *Motivation — Resistance*
Motivation high if anxiety and pain pronounced. Recurrent resistance because of the stress of change.

13. *Transferences — Realities*
Transference *reactions* are explored and differentiated from more accurate reality perceptions through feed-back.

14. *Uniqueness*
Mutual sharing of less desirable parts of self.

sponse there was a series of deliberations by group members which turned the plea for help into an investigation of the phenomenon of "a member's requesting help." In this same log a number of other questions were raised by group members about the meaning of therapy. This view of the therapeutic process declares the force of the group-as-a-whole over the individual to be primary.

Lifton's teachings approach the theme-centered interactional method when he describes the various currents in a group encounter. However, he, like Driver, while recognizing the presence of content, feeling, and interaction, does not seem to be spelling out a holistic, intertwined process. He states (Lifton, p.109):

"As all groups, this one actually moved on three planes simultaneously. One level represents the actual manifest content of the topics they explored. The second level comes from the feelings being expressed through a diversity of content. The last level is represented by the learnings which occur through actual relationships they establish with each other."

In this chapter we have surveyed the everyday, basic terrain of guidance and counseling. From these generally agreed upon sketches we may now build variations, assured that we are rooted in common and mutually understandable constructs.

III

Group
Dynamic
and
Process
Groups

The reader has now viewed groupwork influences mainly from within the counseling discipline. We now face outward — to influences from related professions.

In group counselor education we have found it most useful to focus on two major outside influences: group dynamic and group therapeutic. As the group counselor becomes more aware of his own preferences in style with regard to individual and group dynamics, he will be better prepared to follow the structures and procedures of the TCI system to be presented in Parts Two and Three.

In this chapter we discuss the influences of the T-Group specifically as well as of group dynamics in a more generic sense.

The Laboratory of Small Group Life

The procedures and processes in the present-day T-Group are designed to promote the learning of its members. Most frequently the content to be learned consists of the unfolding group process itself, including individual members' relationship to these here-and-now events. Topics related to the problems or issues which arise in a school, community or organization are another source of content. In the following table, there is a summary of important T-Group features.

A picture of the T-Group in action was provided by Bradford (1964, pp.136-167) in his six episodes culled from different T-Groups. The *group opening* was used by the trainer to explain to the participant that these sessions provide an opportunity to learn more about himself as a functioning member of this group and as a participant in other situations as well. The leader explained that he did not intend to serve as a "group leader." The ensuing anxious reactions of the members — stunned, angered, frustrated — were dealt with by the leader calmly and non-judgementally as he explained that he could not do anything which would make the group more dependent on him.

A *group cleavage* took place within the first several sessions as a result of a split between members. Some believed that maximum learning occurs only when the group works on the immediate problems of "communication, standard setting, and decision making," while other members resisted efforts to understand these group processes — by going off on "safer" topics.

As the ambiguity of the group events grew more apparent, some participants engaged in *private manipulation* as an expression of their power seeking or other asocial designs. This was dealt with by the trainer as a threat to the progress of the group and was exposed by the trainer as an effort at "private manipulation" rather than "public experimentation," thereby preventing a lawless or jungle situation from developing.

In another episode *establishing an effective feedback pattern* was described. Group members recognized the importance of freeing

TABLE 4
T-Groups [1]

1. Definition

A "laboratory method"[2] in which participants are helped to diagnose and experiment with their own and others' responses in groups in a joint learning activity.

2. Theoretical Basis

Group phenomena are not to be understood merely from the point of view of group development or personal dynamics, as they incorporate concepts from many sciences. These include theories of conflict, equilibrium, learning, self-concept, etc.

3. Referral

Self-referred by individuals and organizations.

4. Aims — Benefits

To learn how a group works and how the individual and group affect each other. Benefits are both in personal growth and sensitivity, as well as in improved functioning as a group leader or member.

5. Duration and Composition

Eight to forty hours fitted into days or a few weeks. Eight to twenty members, usually adults ranging widely in age, generally within the same professional, cultural, and intellectual orbit.

6. Ground Rules

Group members responsible for learning about unfolding group processes.

7. *Content*	Group processes; individual's relationship to these processes; individual's sensitivity to his own feelings and style of participation; applications to school, community, and organization.
8. *Special Nature of Experience*	Provides opportunity for mature, productive, and sound relationships among people.
9. *Stages — Sequences*	Dependency-hostility phase (emphasis on power); middle phase where group develops its own history and culture (emphasis on affection and interdependence); ending phase where behavior of group comes through as coordinated and goal directed (emphasis on consensual validation).
10. *Leader*	"Trainer" is neither like teacher, discussion leader, or full member. He intervenes permissively to help members analyze the events; he may re-affirm purpose of group, clarify or interpret group action, and suggest ways of self-study.
11. *Member*	Members responsible for establishing their own way of working, ana-lyzing their problems, and making decisions; are encouraged to experi-ment with and examine their errors and the accuracy of their sensitivity to others.
12. *Motivation — Resistance*	Resistance is high in early stages, but once overintellectualization, over-affective behavior, and selective inattention are reduced, involvement is maximized.

13. *Transferences —Realities*

Reality is maximized through efforts of leader to be openly himself and to encourage this undefensiveness in others.

14. *Uniqueness*

A method which effectively deals with giving and receiving feed-back; study of authority, dependency, and interdependency; developing of structure for problem solving; integration of "cold" work attitudes and emotionality.

[1] In recent years, T-Group trainers have incorporated elements of "process groups" described below, pages 63ff.

[2] Bradford, L.P., Gibb, J.R., Benne, K.D., *T-Group Theory and Laboratory Method*, New York: John Wiley and Sons, 1964, p.1.

and modifying the behavior of individuals to enhance the development of the group. But they were both intrigued and frightened
about receiving frank impressions of themselves from the others. To
help find a way out of the impasse, the trainer undertook a half-hour
presentation of an event in his own life. As the others responded, the
trainer asked for and received help about certain aspects of the presented episode. The group then understood better how feedback
could be effectively controlled and used.

Building a work organization was a slow and complex task.
Gradually the group realized that traditional rules of organization
could not be agreed upon and were not working. With the trainer
frequently focussing on what was going on, a semblance of organization developed. Two subgroups competed for the support of a
middle group representing the bulk of the members. The two camps
represented differences in tolerance for lack of structure, fears about
the results of feedback, and attitudes about the authority of the
trainer. Gradually, as the trainer encouraged the group to keep scanning and evaluating the happenings in the group, a more effective
work-organization emerged.

During the last few sessions most groups moved toward the
ending phase. Usually a feeling of unity was high. Members spoke of
using their T-Group experiences in the future. Often an unresolved
personal problem which had remained encapsulated was thrust forward by the unsatisfied member. Frequently there were "special"
members who inappropriately sought therapeutic help from a T-
Group and who required ongoing or follow-up counseling.

Gradually and inevitably it was recognized that the effects of a
T-Group experience on the person were just as significant as the
effects on the group. Garwood highlighted the outcome for the
individual as including "steps in fundamental growth comparable to
those sought in psychotherapy."

Concerning the impact of the T-Group on the individual, Durkin
drew conclusions about the differences between therapy and training methods at Bethel. She noted that there was no attempt made to
explore the origin of a person's problem, and only interpersonal feelings of the immediate sessions were subject to comment. Rather
that *therapy* taking place, one could describe a *"therapeutic
change"* in an individual which in turn affected and changed the
group or system.

T-Group Applications in Schools

Group guidance workers helped students in their planning and decision making in educational and vocational development and personal adjustment. Now the T-Group influenced group guidance practice by demonstrating ways of preserving and energizing the effective working forces of a group. Of further enrichment were the methods used to train the student in the intellectual and emotional skills needed to become a valued member of a valued group.

The influence of the T-Group on group counseling so far is not so much in its direct application to students but in its use in counselor education. Supervisors and counselor candidates have been placed in the same T-group to help them learn about each other and themselves, get feedback about their social impact, and become more sensitive to complexities of human relationships. The widespread use of groups in counselor education was documented by Pierson (1965) in his visits to twenty-three NDEA Counseling and Guidance Institutes when he described T-Group approaches. He reported that "theories were discussed in connection with interactions within the group. Group process was often stopped . . . and examined. Process was used frequently to clarify basic concepts in counseling and guidance and to give meaning to important theories of human behavior."

Considering the demonstrated value and the widespread influence of the "training group" experience, we may safety assume that many group counselors have been exposed to T-Groups and have attempted to incorporate this method into their own. In all probability the T-Group has had a general impact on counseling by providing both students and counselors with a "group experience" aimed at developing greater personal awareness and sensitivity.

Why, however, have counselors delayed in adapting the learnings from T-Groups (and group dynamics) to their own work with pupils? Upon his return from an invigorating experience in Bethel, Maine (one of the centers of the National Training Laboratories), the group counselor feels that he has something new and special to contribute. But this contribution is not simply a matter of conducting sensitivity and encounter groups in the way he experienced them as a member. He has returned with two complicated problems. One is that if he wants to amplify his group work, he has to compose his own score combining the T-Group method with what he used to do in counseling. He cannot lead a T-Group in one session (with its emphasis upon decision making, cooperative efforts, and research on process), followed in the second session by a counseling group (with its stress upon psychological problem solving and ego-fulfillment). Unifying these two elements requires skill and artistry of a high order. It is not our purpose in this presentation to provide detailed suggestions about unifying the T-Group and the counseling group. However, a combination of the two is illustrated.

A group counselor organizes ten high school seniors who had been looking for summer jobs as camp counselors. They wanted to know more about "leadership" before applying for their positions. They agree to attend five T-Group sessions on studying and practicing effective leadership. It becomes evident to all at the third session that many members are expressing doubt about their ability to develop the skill of leadership. The group counselor suggests at the fourth session — and the idea is readily accepted — that there be another series of five sessions where the members will have group counseling. Here the goal would be to identify the nature of the leadership problem for individuals and to trace its causes and related manifestations in past and present experience.

There is a second problem for the counselor who seeks to adapt his T-Group learnings. The very act of integrating these "socio group" and "psycho group" processes (Coffey, 1964) tends to minimize the boundaries between education, guidance, and counseling. While this fusion may yield valuable results for certain groups, there are other situations which require a more clear-cut approach along stricter lines of guidance, counseling, consultation, or therapy. Here we are reminded of tasks which require briefer teaching guidance emphasis, such as orienting pupils to a new school or an elementary school counselor's being asked to form a children's group to express and exchange feelings about achieving poorly. That in these situations it is helpful to maintain distinct techniques was recommended by Goldman (1962). He cautioned those who do guidance and counseling to utilize the most suitable combination of process and content so as not to confuse the functions of teaching, guidance, counseling, and therapy at any one given time.

Thus when group counselors have been exposed to the T-Group experience, their new wealth can easily become an embarrassment of riches when they return to their schools. They have inherited two new problems. One is how to diversify and nourish their work with new streams of thought from the training group experience. The second is how to preserve their specific roles in educating, guiding, counseling, and consulting when expected and necessary in light of their new multidimensional functioning.

T-Group and TCI Group: Contrasts

A brief comparison of the T-Group method and the TCI seems to be in order here. One major difference lies in the purpose of the group experience. T-Group theory emphasizes educating and training the person for the sake of shaping a well-functioning group. Somewhat at variance is the TCI emphasis which promotes the human being as benefitting by and learning to do things in groups. Hence the T-Group is individual-qua-group-member centered, while TCI is centered on both individual and group.

A second contrast between T-Groups and TCI's is the relative height of human development toward which each is striving. The former is based initially — and this slant remains — on *remedying* education, *improving* the faulty working parts of a group. Our system is based on a model of the person which seeks a higher level of refinement in differentiation and integration and their relating to others. Even when group interaction is moving well, we seek more of authentic dyads *within* the group.

Far removed from classical psychoanalytic contributions, T-Group trainers stress the present as the desired and expected content of importance. In our system we too encourage the pursuit of relevant and reflected preserved learning in the here and now. But we welcome the fitness of then-and-there responses; this can help safeguard that the whole person not be slighted.

Group Dynamics: Uses and Benefits

Group dynamics is a term first used by Kurt Lewin, who, along with other social scientists in the 1930's, began collecting data on group behavior. They were interested in the institution of the group, its processes, and the mutual effects of individuals and group on each other. The T-Group Laboratory Method was one outgrowth of this interest.

While somewhat vague and broad in its definition, group dynamics may be understood (Durkin, p.24) as

> "that field of specialization which is interested in increasing our knowledge of group life, of its processes, its special phenomena, and its particular laws, and in the practical application of this knowledge . . . Group dynamicists continued to define the group as a structure that emerges from individuals in constant dynamic interaction with one another."

Sharing an interest in group dynamics are the following people: social scientists interested in the nature of groups and interactions of its members; business and governmental organizations concerned with the application of human relations skills important for their management problems; teachers and other school personnel who want to use what can be learned of group behavior to provide education in a consistently democratic and cooperative spirit.

Group dynamic processes can be looked at as observable phenomena irrespective of the intrapsychic vicissitudes of specific individuals. Thus from a group dynamics point of view, for example, we can observe that the "missing member" (who is absent or has resigned from the group) always has an impact on a functioning group. But through the eyes of a group counselor, the universality of the missing member's impact on the group is less important than is the specific intrapsychic and interpersonal effect on each individual participant. The group dynamics point of view is scientific in the sense of describing and evaluating group phenomena which could be termed "thing-people." The group counselor's point of view is personal and descriptive, (and "scientific" in his research activity), viewing group process more in intrapsychic terms.

Group Dynamic Links to Group Counseling

Is group dynamics noxious to therapeutic groups — one extreme point of view — or conversely is it at the very heart of counseling and therapy in groups? This question has generally been avoided by counselors. Specific references by *group counselors* to the part played by *group dynamics* in their theory and practice are rare. We can begin to clarify this vexing question by conceptualizing the influence of group dynamics on group counseling in three levels.

At the *first level,* group dynamics is viewed as a rock-bottom condition common to all "social influence" situations. This is a view of group dynamics which points to social factors influencing a group member. Whether it be a prison, kindergarten, or picket line, we are positive that the presence of others influences the individual in some way. This view represents a process which is neither used directly nor ignored. Like topography on a hike, it is recognized and understood but is not generally an intrinsic part of the walk. We know that influencing happens, but we are not that much concerned with the process itself. Specifically, we know that once the counselee has established some sense of security in the group, he feels free to explore threatening thought, feeling, and action which were previously impacted and held back at the expense of a healthy, liberated approach to life. Other examples of underlying, implicit group processes which are "used" by the counselee include validating his perceptions against those of other group participants and rehearsing new behavior within the safety of the group.

The *second level* is the more direct awareness and frequent use of group phenomena and group dynamics in the course of the counseling itself. A group struggling to maintain itself against dissolution is an example of this level.

Finally, at the *third level* there is the direct use of group phenomena for therapeutic effects. The group analyst, therapist, or counselor most influenced by group dynamics sees the very communication itself as providing a therapeutic force. Whether they interpret it in specific group dynamics terms or not, the interpersonal network itself has a built-in therapeutic value. Most typically, the interactions of the members are translated into group dynamics abstractions at the *group level.*

Detailed examples of these three gradations follow.

Level One: Social Influence Concepts

An important attempt to establish a theoretical bond between therapeutic and group dynamics processes was made by Kelman (1963). He seeks to define the barest essentials of "social influence."

The three basic processes which accompany change both within and outside the therapeutic situation are presented as compliance, identification, and internalization. These terms are defined by Kelman:

> *Compliance.* When an individual accepts influence from another person or from a group to attain a favorable reaction . . . or to gain approval;

> *Identification.* When an individual accepts influence from another person or a group in order to establish or maintain a satisfying or self-defining relationship to the others;

> *Internalization.* When an individual accepts influence in order to maintain the congruence of his actions and beliefs with his value system.

Another example of the broad influence of group dynamics is shown by Katz and Lazarsfeld (1955) who drew conclusions about social factors in the individual's behavior as a group member:

1. Benefits which befall the individual who conforms to group norms . . .
2. The individual's dependence on others about him for the definition of "social reality" . . .
3. Interaction . . . operates to produce shared standards of judgement, opinions, and ways of behaving . . .
4. Groups of people demand conformity of individual members to maintain the status of the group . . .

A conclusion drawn by Katz and Lazarsfeld therefore suggests "*group change* as the 'target' for initiating individual attitude and behavior changes."

Frequently overlooked is Freud's description of the group as a dynamic whole with its specific overriding influence upon every individual in the group. He concluded that through a form of identification group members came together in their common aim. Then, having given up their own ideal, they substituted the group ideal as embodied in the father or leader of the horde.

Level Two: Using Group Phenomena

On the following pages are examples of various ways in which group processes are viewed by counselors and therapists. We will see how efforts are made either to borrow, redefine, or integrate group dynamics concepts in relation to the practice of group counseling and group therapy.

One of the established variations of group counseling known as "multiple counseling," a term coined by C.P. Froehlich, is oriented toward group dynamics. The method makes use of a common, cohesive problem and the concept of a democratic leader. Other facets of group dynamics principles in this system are evaluation by group members of group pressure and their identifying with group standards to achieve personal goals. Driver's work along these lines has already been mentioned in Chapter II as an example of multidimensional counseling.

Fullmer and Bernard (1964) describe the "mechanics of the process of a structured group" as consisting of various steps beginning with agreement on a task by counselor and group, including differing reactions by individuals to the discussion, and culminating with the efforts made "to achieve a synthesis of ideas already presented or to bring out new ideas." The bulk of the ensuing description pertains largely to group-determined reactions of counselees in a personal counseling milieu and includes evolving levels of content from the superficial to the intimate. These authors describe group counseling in terms of helping the student to understand his own functioning by way of a group task.

Durkin (1964, pp.26-30) was one of the first to translate the vocabulary of group dynamics and group therapy into terms which make it possible for those who practice in these areas to understand and even reconcile the two approaches. In the following table, six group phenomena are viewed in parallel with applications to group dynamics and group therapy.

Durkin later concludes by suggesting an ingenious reconciliation between group dynamics and group psychoanalytic abstractions (Durkin pp.101-103). Her key to the possible equivalencies summarized in the table below is that "the group dynamic abstractions deal with the *result* of any given behavioral interaction while the psychoanalytic abstractions deal with its *cause.*"

TABLE 5

Group Dynamics Phenomena Significant for Psychotherapy

Factor	Group Dynamics	Group Therapy
Group goal or decision	Group as a whole has a common problem-solving goal.	Only the leader is in touch with the major goals for the individuals.
Original group atmosphere	Cooperative	Permissiveness takes precedence over co-operativeness
Self-oriented needs	Works against group movement	Group thrives on these because resolving ego-centric needs is first step in working together.
Leadership	Preoccupation with democratic leadership as well as identification by leader with group to find ways of influencing its members.	Realistic, authoritative, but not authoritarian position. Democratic attitudes emerge in the form of non-verbal respectfulness to members.
Cohesiveness	The more cohesive the group, the more the norms of its members are affected.	Togetherness is good up to a point. Beyond this it becomes too safe and gratifying.
Structure	Interaction, an important aspect of structure, is a product of the members' motivation and serves the purpose of reducing tension and dissension.	A product of the members' behavior and attitudes which in turn are either accepted or rejected by the others in terms of achieving the particular goal at a given time.

TABLE 6

Possible Equivalencies between
Group Dynamics and Group Psychoanalysis

Group Dynamics Terms (*effects*)	*Group Psychoanalytic Terms* (*causes*)
Resonance	Acting in transference
Cohesiveness	Identification and libidinal ties
Disruptive factors	Aggressive factors
Submissiveness	Transference to group as a whole, either as Oedipal father or pre-Oedipal mother
Subgrouping	Interlocked neurotic needs are dove-tailed
Scapegoating	Transference between masochist and group member from whom he elicits sadism

Coinciding with Durkin's view that group dynamics concepts may be adapted for therapy, Andrews (1962) provides a clear example of six group dynamics which may be used as facilitating agencies for effective therapy. These dynamics fall into areas or categories which are of equal interest to the group dynamicist and group therapist.

Andrews makes it quite clear at the start that it is the individual and not the group who is the subject of therapy. Andrews' first dynamic in his mothers' group is *group balance.* He seeks to balance the "instigators" and "isolates" to provide a well-balanced structural property. Next in the category of group goals he describes the second dynamic, *group task orientation*, which is his way of having the mothers in the group relate to their membership in an "emotionally honest" way. The encouragement of *universalization* — sharing of common personality characteristics and problems — is a third dynamic. *Extensive emotional support* is a fourth. The final two dynamics are in the category of group pressures. The fifth dynamic is *defense confrontation,* where the dissolving of defenses is facilitated by group members and leader. The sixth is *experimental validation,* defined as more appropriate behavior.

Studying one important ubiquitous group force, "conformity," Bonney (1965) apprises us of the various dimensions of this process. Without even aiming to do so, the counselor benefits from the trend toward conformity. Pressures toward uniformity help keep a group oriented toward developing and maintaining a therapeutic atmosphere; the tendency of group members to seek agreement on emotional and social reality enables the individual member to find consensual or social validation for his individual opinion. But the conformity force does not always yield the best product. A counselor may be misled by the sudden increased verbalization of a person who has been too withdrawn. This change may merely reflect a "me too" attitude, a sort of transitory "conformity cure." We may add this to the list of "transference cures" and "flights into health." In this context Bonney also reminds us that reactions to being part of a group-conformity situation vary from one individual to the next. In view of all these facts, the group counselor can adopt a broader frame of reference for perceiving rebellious behavior. A counselee may not necessarily be rebelling against or resisting a transferential figure, but he may be opposing pressures to conform. If resistances were noted in many of the members at one time, it is possible again that (instead of or in addition to a series of individual resistive reactions) we are dealing with an "adherence to a group norm of which the counselor is unaware." This analysis of "conformity dynamics" within the context of counseling demonstrates an important point of contact between the two disciplines, providing added meaning to the concept of conformity.

Some have found it more useful to deal with the group dynamics or group therapy issue by using the term "group phenomena," in effect minimizing the difference. Kadis et al. refer to "G-responses" which are "various central response situations having occurred often enough to be identifiable as unique and indigenous to the therapy group . . . It is likely to be a kind of homeostatic response which has as its goal the maintenance of whatever level of anxiety the group can sustain." A common homeostatic response is that of the group members who resist the therapist's changing the status quo. Other examples of this G-response are mentioned as multiple transferences (to various members as well as to the therapist), reactive associations (to the specific interpersonal setting of the group), defense mechanisms (which support group members' resistance to change), acting out toward other group members (for the underlying purpose of changing the group homeostasis), and subgrouping (as a means of becoming insulated from therapy and the therapist).

Level Three: Group Process as Therapy

At the third level of group dynamics effects on group therapy are the "group-oriented" group therapists who say that group process virtually *is* group therapy. In the British Army during World War II, Bion treated groups of combat fatigue cases by showing the soldiers how their tensions and anxieties prevented them from working as a group. The cure was to take place only as the group worked better together.

Cartwright's principles for achieving change in group members, quoted by Lifton (p.205), may be considered as representative of those who advocate the use of group as the primary force for individual modification.

"1. If the group is to be used effectively as a medium of change, those people who are to be changed and those who are to exert influence for change must have a strong sense of belonging to the same group.
2. The more attractive the group is to its members, the greater is the influence that the group can exert on its members.
3. In attempts to change attitudes, values, or behavior, the more relevant they are to the basis of attraction to the group, the greater will be the influence that the group can exert upon them.
4. The greater the prestige of a group member in the eyes of the other members, the greater the influence he can exert.
5. Efforts to change individuals or subparts of a group which, if successful, would have the result of making them deviate from the norms of the group, will encounter strong resistance.
6. Strong pressure for changes in the group can be established by creating a shared perception by members of the need for change, thus making the source of pressure for change lie within the group.
7. Information relating to the need for change, plans for change, and consequences of change must be shared by all relevant people in the group.
8. Changes in one part of a group produce strain in other

related parts which can be reduced only by eliminating the change or by bringing about readjustments in the related parts."

Lakin and Dobbs (1962) specifically studied the therapeutic effects of group phenomena. Described were processes which included a *pairing reaction* disrupted by an *attention seeker;* a *group standard* was tentatively accepted by group members other than the *attention seeker;* the pattern of deviancy of one of the group members was highlighted. The authors of the case suggest that "the discovery of the effects upon different individual patients of the different group processes may lead to a more precise articulation of what may be therapeutic and what may be non-therapeutic in group psychotherapy."

There are fully developed methods which combine group dynamics with group psychoanalysis, such as those practiced by S.H. Foulkes, W.R. Bion, and H. Ezriel. These are described by Durkin (1964, p.313) as perceiving

the therapy group in terms of the three basic tenets of Lewinian field theory. (1) They treat the group as an entity (a system in tension), look for the latent meaning of its interaction, and consistently formulate their interventions in relation to it. (2) Its energy is considered to derive from the tension created by the needs of the members (parts) in interaction (in their struggle for life space) and to give rise to the group processes . . . harnessed by the leader for therapeutic purposes. (3) By focusing chiefly on the immediate group events they put the principle of contemporaneity into practice. . . .

Several other group therapists and analysts have developed important links with group dynamics. J.L. Moreno, a pioneer in sociometry, also uses group process as a basis for his psychodrama in which groups of patient-actors receive therapy through the spontaneity and creativity of interpersonal conflict drama. The method of Bach was described by Durkin (1964) as focusing elements of Lewin, Freud, and Bion and utilizing techniques of role playing, art, and projective techniques. The Adlerians, stressing a holistic approach, have always postulated "social interest" as a core concept. It is within the group that the individual best learns of his faulty perceptions and how to correct them.

The Chickens or the Egg?

Let us rephrase this question more seriously: "Which factor is given more weight by the group leader in his work with the group, the group or the individual member?" The answer to this question will characterize the degree to which the group worker is more individual or group oriented. It will say something about whether the leader considers the participant from the point of individual personality dynamics or group dynamics. Does the leader see the participant developing himself so as to build a better group, or is the group there as a means of building a better individual? We discuss these issues in the context of the therapeutic group worker.

However hesitant he may be because of the complexities of "bringing in the group," or focusing on the individual, the group counselor soon begins to develop some initial preference or allegiance along the continuum of individual-oriented/group-oriented approaches. At one end, Wolf and Schwartz believe that group dynamics by itself is not therapeutic and should not be elevated as a "mystique." The group forces described by group dynamicists are viewed by these authors as winds of resistance which blow therapy off course. These authors state their preference for doing *psychoanalysis in groups.*

In an intermediate position is the group counselor who frequently employs individual counseling interventions. He may also use group dynamics concepts, such as encouraging the group to build a cooperative "group climate." The pitfall sometimes found here is a lack of consistency and plan, an overgrown-garden effect, where the counselor deals at random with the individual, interactions, and group movement.

At the other end of the scale is the counselor who aligns himself with the concept of group as *the* therapeutic force. He would agree with Foulkes (1965) that just as the neuron is related to the network of the nervous system, so is the individual bound indivisibly to the group and its configuration. This counselor would focus on the "group response" and consider it primary.

No matter where he is on the scale, the counselor interested in applying group dynamics principles builds on those aspects of process which have value for counseling. The counselor introducing the concept of "roles" in his group finds that several members for the first time experience their own actions more insightfully. But caution is needed to prevent the use of group dynamics terms from slipping into a study of how a group is structured through the roles of its members, thereby weakening the intended purpose of the counselor.

Another example of group dynamics forces relevant to counseling is the leader's employment of process to enhance freedom of interaction. In a high school group two co-counselors discovered that their informal leadership was inhibiting effective group interaction. Resistance remained at a high level. The students complained about "adults' manipulating and contriving." The leadership process was mishandled, as the adults were not as readily accepted as they had hoped. The group members eventually responded better to a more formal structuring wherein the leaders acted less as participants than they normally would have in conducting an adult group.

The Experiential Current

In groupwork today there is confusion mixed with excitement about new combinations of theory and practice from the "group explosion" of this decade. Some of these new emphases now flavor groupwork sessions with "minilabs," encounters, sensitivity, confrontation techniques, body awareness, and marathons. The hallmark of these elements is immediate sensory and emotional expression, accompanied by heightened self-awareness.

The "group process experience" (Berger 1968) with highly motivated and strongly committed individuals moves toward intensive exchanges helped by cohesiveness and growing mutual trust. People join to learn about themselves by way of encounter, through a participatory study of the unfolding interactions. The group process member is invited on stage in a drama for which living encounter provides the script. The actor is asked to present himself in a way that will enhance the living experience. He does so by taking a series of timely risks. He is not required by the leader to shed more than a layer or two of his protective facade. Indeed, it would often be inadvisable for more of this stripping away to happen. In a culture they perceive as being run more and more by machines, the students want to feel more human, at ease, and at one with their peers. The fruit of such sessions could not only help develop pockets of spontaneity and honesty among subgroups at school but also engender a full feeling of gratitude toward peers and adults whom they have experienced in a new way.

It is difficult to generalize about the degree of personal involvement by the leaders: some are *with* the group, others do things *to* the group. By mining such rich lodes of ore as gesture, voice, and movement and encouraging reciprocal actions and reactions of the members, the "group process" leader serves to bring to the surface (and makes socially available) forgotten or unassimilated parts of the self. The Gestalt approach deserves a much fuller treatment in terms of its sometimes remarkable breakthroughs enabling patients to make the component parts of their conflict recognizable, palpable, and balanced in the field and ground of their functioning selves. Here we wish only to mention its connection with process groups because of the emphasis upon bringing out the unconscious as the source of concealed powers which man has for a liberated, creative, fully involved life with others.

In process groups, distorted reactions to the leaders and other group members are not developed and analyzed as "transferential reactions" to be viewed microscopically as products of conditionings at an early age. Rather the member is helped to clear up the blur in his perception of the next person by exploring his immediate reactions to this person as well as by using the "consensual validations" of others in terms of their reactions. Transference analysis is given second place to developing in a more immediate sense the skill of intuition and open, responsible, interaction with others. If Harry senses that Joan, sitting nearby in a group process experience, has a stingy, withholding quality in what she has to offer, this feeling may be based more on reality than transference. The well-timed, constructive use or transmission of this intuition by members and leader may well result in an experience of great moment for Harry and Joan. Harry has finally recognized and dealt with female withholding, not as debilitating rejection aimed at him necessarily but as behavior he could deal with assertively and objectively. Joan at long last finally experienced a true, caring, and undefensive reaction to her fearful holding back. This encounter permitted both participants to feel the strength of unused feelings and reactions.

Resistances are present in group process experiences but not in the highly charged form noted in therapeutic groups. By definition, the group process member is less defensive about the prospect of *change* and less concerned with revealing *pathology.* Even though his initial anxiety level may be high, the group process member may soon feel at ease, carried along by the enthusiasm and earnest participation of the others.

Working through a major obstacle to development or a conflict in the form of a symptom or character trait is not a major goal for the group process member. He rather builds on his self-awareness, inter-actional skills, or some other goals, depending upon the aim and mood of the group. He plunges first into the group experience itself and derives secondarily certain therapeutic dividends which accrue as a result of increased intellectual and emotional freedom and intel-lectual clarity.

We feel as does Berger (1968);

"The amount of feeling expressed concerning termination is phenomenal. There is much open appreciation, gratitude, and reaching toward others. Highly-cohesed groups often go through a verbalized, deeply-felt mourning phase prior to saying farewell . . . this is not only based on separation anxiety but sadness because a rich emotional experience is coming to an end."

The TCI approach recognizes the existence and presence of many processes, such as group climate, leadership, subgroups, scape-goating, and group pressure for conformity. But we do not aim to work with them in any focal way, with the exception of those occasions when they emerge strongly and we deal with them frankly in passing. More central is our emphasis on process which moves con-tinuously from one end of the "individual-group" scale to the other, where the focus is on the person's growth in the context of giving and taking with others. More specific statements of TCI group process may be found in Chapters VI, VII, and X.

A study of the following table will serve to summarize the con-tent of the section on process groups.

TABLE 7

Process and Encounter Groups

1. *Definition*	To share openly individual and interpersonal responses as they emerge in the immediate experience. Emphasis is on sensory and emotional expression.
2. *Theoretical Basis*	To grow by developing one's capacities for self-expression is to become alive, more actualized, and more human.
3. *Referral*	Self-referral. Desire for growth, stimulation, and variety of interactive experiences. Disruptive or disturbed applicants are screened out.
4. *Aims — Benefits*	Learning (mainly affectively) in the here-and-now about living with and experiencing oneself and others more deeply and fully.
5. *Duration and Composition*	Almost anyone not in the midst of a serious problem or not seriously disturbed; from four hours to three weeks. Eight to twenty members, or more.
6. *Ground Rules*	Act, transact, emote, sense, release repression.
7. *Content*	All manifestations of living in a framework of honesty, openness, and responsibility.
8. *Special Nature of Experience*	The immediate impact of using one's powers of feeling, sensation, and

perception for satisfaction and growth.

9. *Stages — Sequences*

Individually and collectively, movement toward growth proceeds (after initial anxiety and confusion) in this sequence: trust, openness, realization, emergence, or interdependence (Gibb and Gibb). [1]

10. *Leader*

To require no less openness, self-revelation, and intimacy than expected of the members; must guard against unlicensed or sadistic behavior in name of frankness. Some leaders use techniques not calling for their personal participation.

11. *Member*

Experiencing and risking change and impact of the emerging processes.

12. *Motivation — Resistance*

High motivation. Members join in the hope of learning and gratification. Resistance can often be masked.

13. *Transferences — Realities*

Transferences are not dealt with directly, but they are continuously being formed and dissolved in the intense give and take of the experience. The fluidity and generally positive quality of the interactions result in behavioral experimentation which tends to resolve some transferences in the light of reality.

14. *Uniqueness*

Rapid development of sharing, caring, and trusting. Confrontations are frequent, potent, and revelatory experiences binding people together for the duration of the group.

[1]Gibb, J.R. and Gibb, L.M. "Humanistic Elements in Group Growth," in J.F.T. Bugental (Ed.), *Challenges of Humanistic Psychology*, New York: McGraw-Hill, 1967.

IV

Group
Therapy
Influences

Group counselors, inundated by the subtly damaging influences of war, poverty, and pollution on personality growth in the schools, welcome whatever effective tools they can find and use. In Chapter III we suggested ways of enhancing group counseling and group guidance through the introduction of group dynamics. Here we do the same with respect to group therapeutic influences.

The general tendency has been for the group counselor to avoid direct connections with group therapy theory and practice. This avoidance is understandable for historical and pragmatic reasons related to the intimate connection between counselor and school. The school is for learning, not "curing." Yet it is unmistakably clear that with decades of growth of psychotherapy and counseling, cross-cultural exchanges did take place. In this chapter we wish to assist the group counselor in recognizing, developing, and defining his own style and function in terms of various influences from psychotherapeutic and psychoanalytic practice.

As a result of cross-fertilization, the overwhelming opinion today is that (group) counseling and (group) therapy are alike in almost every respect, differing only in certain less important distinctions, such as severity of disturbance and treatment setting (Patterson). A minority opinion (Slavson, 1966) finds that there are clear distinctions in aims and dynamics. However, even these distinctions break down in actual practice, where "pure" forms rarely exist.

In the presence of such converging and overlapping in therapy and counseling, the task of isolating "group therapeutic influences" is made more difficult. If group counseling practice does tend to take the form of a chemical compound in which "group therapeutic influences" — among others — have been mixed, special care is needed to trace and identify these tendencies. A full treatment of this would require an historical study of its own. Our purpose here is to survey two of the broad, definable currents or "group therapeutic influences" which have provided a source of nourishment for the theory and practice of group counseling. We observe that the group counselor has found ways to

1. Intensify his therapeutic contact;
2. Expand the scope of his technical practice to encompass a greater variety of situations with a broader school population.

The Counselor's Work in Depth

Intensifying the counseling contact for the group counselor, the unconscious becomes the road to *deepening* his therapeutic contact. He had been perched at the edge of the forbidden land, beyond the reach of Freudian concepts such as dream interpretation, transference, ego, and superego. Psychoanalytic influence was so shunned that even Adlerian principles (with emphasis upon man's striving for socialization), practiced in unmistakable "group counseling" terms a half century ago, did not readily find their way explicitly into current counseling. Among other instances of avoiding the unconscious was Rank's emphasis upon the goal of separation and independence, a theory of potential value to counselors which has been only dimly perceived and weakly integrated by counselors in their work with groups.

Yet gradually the group counselor accepted the challenge of enlarging and refining theory and technique in the light of commonly accepted psychotherapeutic practice. While not articulating his practice in Freudian terms, the group counselor became aware of the benefit of releasing the ego — which was bound by anxiety and guilt — through a clarification of underlying conflicts in a supportive, communicative group setting. Focus on prevailing defense mechanisms of group members as a defense against anxiety — technically a thrust into unconscious areas of the ego — became a familiar and useful intervention. The group counselor learned that superego demands could be reduced by universalization, which in turn was enhanced by structuring the group along more homogeneous lines. He noted that pent-up aggressions — within bounds — could be successfully released with his modifying and guiding activity. The release and liberation of repressed thoughts and feelings were noted to have a direct bearing on the increased flow of energy for creative learning and expression. Budding transferential reactions were utilized as live demonstrations of the group members' broader relationships with family members and significant others — without the necessity of cultivating and analyzing fully flowered "transference neuroses."

We have no idea about the frequency of these therapeutic interventions; an investigation of such influences in the sample protocols by counseling practitioners would be required for an accurate estimate. But certainly many group counselors will hear a familiar ring in the principles given above, which flow from the basic characteristics of psychoanalytic therapy. Scheidlinger (1963) lists these "generic, interrelated elements: (1) relationship, (2) emotional support, (3) catharsis, (4) reality testing, (5) insight, and (6) reorganization of defensive patterns."

Therapeutic influences are easily identifiable in counselors' notes and transcripts. Glanz's (1962, pp. 285-287) transcript of a college group counseling session, while not designed to illustrate a therapeutic or psychoanalytic orientation, provides us with this very material. In the opening interventions by the counselor (in the seventh out of eight group sessions), we discover a series of therapeutic influences:

1) Counselor provides *emotional support* by telling Connie it

was "a good question" when she asked Karl what his fear
was about talking freely;

2) Counselor builds a *relationship* with Jon in commenting,
"Fearing criticism is pretty common but that doesn't make it
less painful";

3) Counselor encourages Cass, apparently aiming at *catharsis*
by saying, "Give it a try . . . could you talk more about it?";

4) Counselor suggests *reality testing* by saying to Cass, "I feel
your comments are very useful to the group. Why should
you expect me to criticize you? I'm not your father."

5) Counselor works on *reorganization of defensive patterns* in
asking Peggy, "Why hold on to these attitudes?" (that being
criticized by others makes someone bad).

As the counselor absorbed more of these aforementioned group
therapeutic influences, he had to recognize, encourage, and work
with those aspects of the individual which were hitherto unknown or
unexplored. In recent years the trends in counselor education and
professional development have been to prepare the counselor for
new and enlarged dimensions in his functioning by having him
undergo personal counseling sessions as well as "group experiences" of various kinds.

An issue of the *International Journal of Group Psychotherapy*
(October 1967) was devoted to "approaches to training through the
small group." In one article by Zinberg and Friedman (1967), the
authors used a group experience in "teaching college courses in
group and individual dynamics, teaching groups of educators something about events in groups, teaching potential group leaders something about group process, and helping student nurses, physicians,
psychiatric residents and medical students with various aspects of
their professional roles." Such inviting personal growth experiences,
fed and stimulated by group therapy, are on the way to becoming a
part of the training and professional experience of the group counselor in many graduate curricula. The recent trend of making un-
planned use of encounter and "sensitivity" groups as an alternative
to methodical learning experiences is as amorphous in theory as it is
spontaneous in spirit. This trend seems like an inadequate pathway
for group work training.

On the other hand, group supervision in depth provides indispensable "practice-centered" group experience for counselors. In
his counseling practicum Orton (1964) is not satisfied with simple

case presentations where the counselor presents a case and the instructor, aided by the other students of counseling, raises or answers questions about technical processes. He deals rather with four areas of focus: the training agency, the clients being counseled by practicum students, the students themselves, and the dynamics and developments of the supervisory group. The group supervisor shifts the attention of the group from one area to another depending on the directions and problems raised in the counselor presentation. The student cannot help but emerge from such sessions with a deepened awareness of himself not only as a group counselor with technical skills but also as a more integrated thinking, feeling, behaving group participant.

Expanding the Counselor's Work: Therapeutic

There are many students today who are not personally or culturally accessible to the middle-class white counselor trained in the past few decades. Those in ferment include activist blacks who want more of the American pie, young radicals with programs for transforming our society, alienated and uncommitted people who "drop out" from society and go in directions of either more or less personal and social growth. We believe with McGowan (1970) that the counselor can stand in an intermediate position between serving as an agent of society and an agent of the client — to be translator and consultant for these dissident individuals and groups. Many new techniques are needed to perform such a service; the TCI approach is one such possibility. We cannot overemphasize that whatever new services are developed, *the basic counseling, therapeutic, and group dynamics roots which we have traced in detail will prove to have value for the counselor of all seasons* whether in the office, school corridor, classroom, commune, or community.

There are several other fundamental approaches which the counselor needs to apply as he faces the challenge of social change. Three models, products of group therapeutic influence, have already struck roots in schools, social work agencies, clinics, and private practice. These are family therapy (Ackerman, 1966 and Satir, 1964), activity group therapy (Slavson, 1943 and Scheidlinger, 1962), and play group therapy (Axline, 1947 and Ginott, 1961). With moves towards decentralization of school governing boards in urban areas, the gap between home, school, and community is being reduced. Psychological personnel — especially counselors — will be asked to work with students not only as learners in the formal curriculum but also as human beings who grow through living within improved family relationships, functioning in creative play in groups, and undertaking constructive work experience. In this volume we limit our discussion of these group approaches to a tabular summary of their working parts.

Expanding the Counselor's Work: Consultation

Requests for consultation in the school range widely. One variety is represented by a hurried question in the hallway: "What shall we do with Harold, the sixth grader, on Monday?" A more involved consultation would attempt to answer the challenge: "How can we rehabilitate the city educational system with a $50,000 grant earmarked to sensitize teachers, counselors, and administrators?" This question, hopefully, will not be dealt with in a hallway. Whether the data are Harolds or the client a city government, the counselor is being asked to diagnose and recommend courses of action.

If the counselor-consultant requires sagacity —if not audacity — to fulfill his task, the group consultant has an even greater challenge when he employs a more high-powered group consultation approach. His job is to keep the task-centered expediting function of his consultation group alive and moving. He must not be derailed for too long by those consultees in his group who may for a moment mistake their mission to be therapy, a marathon, a lecture, an inquisition, or a search for miracles.

There is no question but that group consultation can affect the widest population with the most good using the least relative energy. The consultation process stretches the counselor's arms far and wide in school and community. The range of opportunity is limited only by the counselor's store of ingenuity in ferreting out the consultation. In a sense he has to create a demand for his own business by keeping a sharp lookout for any opportunity to make clients out of students, teachers, administrators, or parents. Since requests for consultation may involve administrative or working relationships within the consultant's school, counselors from schools at a distance could exchange such services profitably. This exchange would provide the necessary "outside" resource called for in such cases.

TABLE 8

Family Counseling

1. *Definition*	Treating the family as a whole as well as partitioned into its individuals and subgroups.
2. *Theoretical Basis*	The family is a source of destructiveness and growth. Symbiotic and other transferential bonds create an unstable homeostasis which, if dissolved, could make the family a source of strength and health.
3. *Referral*	A family is often brought in through the symptomatology of one of its members.
4. *Aims — Benefits*	To modify the fixed neurotic patterns of interaction; to focus on the family vectors impinging on the individuals; to establish better communications; to expose defensiveness; to clarify the forces which may be victimizing family members.
5. *Duration and Composition*	Members of one (or possibly several) family in various combinations.
6. *Ground Rules*	Speak as freely as possible while respecting others' rights. No physical acting out.
7. *Content*	Identifying and understanding: main problem, patterns of planning, how

parents operate as peers and parents, negative and positive value system of the family directed toward its members, leadership structure, identification processes between parents and children, sociologically related problems, such as delinquency and divorce, which more directly reflect a sick society. (Satir, 1964).

8. *Special Nature of Experience* Recognizing the influence of prevailing intrafamily feelings, attitudes, values, and relationships on one's self as a family member.

9. *Stages — Sequences* Evaluational; working through main problems; terminating.

10. *Leader* Flexibility is paramount because of the variety of subgroup meetings, range of ages, and tendency for members to seek an ally in the therapist. Cotherapists are usually needed.

11. *Member* To be successful, he comes under unusual strain to depart from the usual imbedded, fixed patterns and roles in his family unit.

12. *Motivation — Resistance* Strong motivation by those who are unhappiest in the family. High resistance to change by those who are not being scapegoated.

13. *Transferences — Realities* Typical transferences are reflected in parental expectations of children, symbiotic attachments between parent and child, and lack of complementarity of role between husband and wife. Reality testing of interaction is a vehicle for focusing on misguided and misdirected pursuit of

needs as a family member.

Continuous evaluation and improvement of the network of communication patterns, as the leader declines to take sides or act as omniscient advisor.

14. *Uniqueness*

TABLE 9

Activity and Play Groups

1. *Definition*	Group counseling in the medium of an extracurricular play (including puppetry and psychodrama) or arts and crafts activity.
2. *Theoretical Basis*	"Ego therapy" at the nonverbal level, reproducing the family situation. Self-awareness gained in the action setting, not through interpretation.
3. *Referral*	Wide range of personality and conduct problems.
4. *Aims — Benefits*	More realistic conception of self and environment. Release of guilt, hostility, "safe" expression of love; child more readily accepts counselor's suggestions and comments.
5. *Duration and Composition*	Eight to ten members, grouped according to personality dynamics. On a weekly basis for one and a half hours for a school term or year. Groups are open and continuous. Ages five to fourteen.
6. *Ground Rules*	Be free in self expression; no destroying of property, taking things from another member, or persistent fighting.
7. *Content*	Aggressive, withdrawing, and other kinds of behavior as they emerge through the play and activities.

8. *Special Nature of Experience*

Activity catharsis.

9. *Stages — Sequences*

Early anxiety and distrust followed by increased self-confidence and feelings of belonging. In final stage, activity and play have become more socialized and the degree of withdrawal or violence is diminished.

10. *Leader*

Action interpretation by permissive, supportive leader who must be able to feel unthreatened by and understanding of regressive, challenging, and otherwise erratic or "shocking" behavior.

11. *Member*

Ability to maintain oneself in a peer situation without excessive anxiety and with capacity to accept protection and leadership of the leader.

12. *Motivation — Resistance*

Play and activity catharsis provide intrinsic interest for participants. Resistance by fearful, overaggressive, distrusting, and symbiotic children.

13. *Transferences — Realities*

High degree of reality testing. No work with transference reactions.

14. *Uniqueness*

Emotional and physical interaction. Low levels of anxiety. Derivative insight.

In the following table specific features of consultation in groups are discussed.

A unique feature of group consultation — one which is often not understood or carried out — is that the consultant performs most effectively when he enters the "system" from outside the hierarchical organization which seeks his help. If a dean of students were to ask an experienced counselor on his staff to serve as consultant for the adjoining office of student activities on the problem of developing student leadership skills, the subtle and overt complications are apparent: The consultees can hardly feel free to examine their problem undefensively with one who may have unresolved personal and organizational connections with one or more of them. Secondly, the real or fancied professional channels between the counselor-consultant and the dean of students (director of the department which administers student activities), not to mention other faculty members, could hardly be conducive to the airing of complaints toward others in the college hierarchy. Finally the autonomous carrying out of recommendations following the consultation would be hampered if the consultant were actually present (within the organization) observing and judging the effects of the consultation.

At the present stage of development, the counselor as group consultant is most often called upon within his own school. In view of the obvious disadvantages, he is obliged either to operate in a modified way or to arrange for consultations in other schools. A review of the following techniques listed by the Community Mental Health Department of the Postgraduate Center for Mental Health (1960) suggests a number of workable processes for the counselor-group consultant:

> "One, assisting the client-system to discover the nature of problems: collecting data, defining the problem and setting up a problem-solving plan; two, enhancing the problem-solving skills of the individuals in the groups within the client system; three, opening up communication channels within the client-system and handling the effects of feedback; four, helping to implement the plan within the client-system; five, handling the resistances to change and learning (maintaining a proper relationship with the status levels of the client-system); six, helping the client-system to obtain the proper 'outside' resources when these are

TABLE 10

Group Consultation

1. *Definition*	Enhancing knowledge, broadening skills, and dealing with specific problems of an organization by a consultant for the consultee.
2. *Theoretical Basis*	Focused fact finding and skilled intervention by a consultant trained in education, behavioral sciences, and individual and group dynamics can help facilitate change and growth in individuals and organizations.
3. *Referral*	Request made by key personnel in an organization.
4. *Aims — Benefits*	To provide a diagnosis and recommended program of improvement.
5. *Duration and Composition*	With key personnel, staff personnel, and those serviced by the consultants, usually for a limited period of days or weeks at the site of the organization or agency.
6. *Ground Rules*	To engage in the consultation process in good faith, trusting the constructive intent and sharing freely with the consultant outsider.
7. *Content*	Example with teachers: understanding classroom interactions and one's personal relationships with pupils, understanding practical use of

sensitivity, self-awareness, relating to parents.

8. *Special Nature of Experience*

Applications of counseling, group work, mental health, educational and sociological principles to improvement.

9. *Stages — Sequences*

Entry or exploratory; problem-solving and working relationship; withdrawal and evaluation of service.

10. *Leader*

Mature, judicious approach to problems of an organization, utilizing training as counselor, but supplementing this with knowledge of related professions and problem-solving, expediting group techniques.

11. *Member*

Willingness to participate with others in the same organization in frank personal exchanges about the program and work.

12. *Motivation — Resistance*

Frequent objections to the "outsider" brought in by administrators to "inspect" and make changes. But strong motivation if consultees were part of the original planning and decision to get the consultant.

13. *Transferences — Realities*

Consultant aims at improving everyday communications among the consultees, using reality as a base.

14. *Uniqueness*

Consultees ask what they can do about *others* by way of exploring and then taking action.

indicated; seven, training the supervisory staff to carry on with the training, both in terms of skills and information; eight, withdrawal from the client-system."

Since we agree that the counselor-group consultant is in danger of diffusing and confusing his role when identified with the same "system" as the consultee, it is suggested that any clear cut consultation problems related to his own school be avoided. Examples of realistic areas in Caplan's terms (1961) are: (1) "client-centered case consultation" in which the primary goal is change in the client (the student); (2) "consultee-centered case consultation" where the primary goal is change in the consultee (administrators, teachers or parents).

One kind of "client-centered case consultation" would involve the entry of the counselor-consultant into the "system" of a group of teachers who seek assistance in teacher-child or teacher-class relationships. Primarily these eight or so teachers are asking what they can do about *others* and only secondarily what they can do about themselves. They want to *explore* and to know what *action* they can take to increase their effectiveness in the classroom. If this desire is the teachers' aim, the consultant seeks to bring to life within the group a series of interactions and cognitive case discussions which will concretize the kinds of pathological and unadaptive pupil and teacher behavior leading to problems in the classroom.

The authors agree with Boris (1967, p.46; p.50) that "The major thrust is toward revivifying the material brought in from outside through intensifying it in such a way as to produce identification with it." Interference with the task of examining the emerging material in the consultative process is understood in the same light as resistance to any change, or perhaps too as confusion resulting from distorted orientation toward the task of teaching. As in therapy, the group consultant seeks to evoke, in L. K. Frank's phrase, the teacher's "inner speech, governing his life, which is unproductive and of which he is unaware." Whatever the conceptual and theoretical orientation of the group consultant, his method invariably would include introduction of demonstrable material by way of group process, case presentation, role playing, and topics such as empathy with another generation and self-expectations as a teacher.

Since revelations and interpretations of consultees' behavior by the group consultant-counselor are avoided, the teachers in the group go through an initial stage of both gaining mastery and resenting the consultant for frustrating their wishes to be "good and dependent." Following this stage, the consultant continues to encourage a working and cohesive attitude by recognizing important group themes and by highlighting indications of personality strength shown by individuals. The end product of this model of group consultation is the termination of the experience after a previously agreed upon number of sessions usually ranging from five to fifteen, each being one to two hours in length. After a successful experience, the consultees leave with a feeling that they have achieved self-renewal. They have structured for themselves "authentic" guidelines for functioning in their professions.

The Theme-Centered Interactional System as a New Arrival

TCI as a newcomer to group work partakes of certain qualities of group dynamics, group therapy, and group education. TCI has benefited from the Zeitgeist which includes the sophistication and documentation of the T-Group laboratory, the scientific study of small-group process by social psychologists and sociologists, and the finely tooled formulations of group psychoanalysts and psychotherapists. Also we have benefited from the work of those who have sought greater congruence between curriculum, method, and living situations in the classroom. Finally we have been inspired by our experience with existential philosophers such as Martin Buber, Paul Tillich, and Ruth C. Cohn, whose writings have helped explain us to ourselves.

In an integrative and innovative way, TCI has provided a patterned and highly flexible system for the interplay of sensory, emotional, and cognitive modes. Through the dynamic balancing of these elements by the leader, each member of the group is encouraged to meet the theme in a spirit of curiosity and desire to use and master relevant knowledge, with an awareness of other individuals moving in like fashion. This experience, which we term "living-learning," is TCI's answer to the challenge of our time: to find a parsimonious theory and a practical method to approach a variety of problems typically found in our world. This task we seek to accomplish in an atmosphere catalytic to the emergence of whole persons.

V

From
Dialogue
to
Group

Introduction

The special emphasis of this chapter is the *counselor in transition,* from individual to group. No doubt many counselors, other professionals and those in community work are engaging in group work without prior training in individual counseling and therapy. Although without strong academic or professional background, they have a lifetime of intuitions and interpersonal sensibilities utilized in leading groups. Calling for more specific requirements, the National Training Laboratories (Bradford, et al., p.478) suggests for "academically based trainers" a strong background in one of the behavioral sciences as well as "a concern for developing his skills in process of application of knowledge to human affairs." In formal counselor and group therapy education, the trend today is to consider leadership of groups as an advanced and more complex training extension of the dyadic relationship.

The group leader in guidance and counseling has been confronted with many exciting, challenging innovations which are easier to read about than to digest and assimilate into his own body of knowledge. The group worker is sometimes puzzled about how to integrate these new developments with his personal-emotional preferences of style, requirements of his job, and theoretical orientation. To achieve a better cognitive grasp of his method, the group worker will find it helpful to rate himself on the following series which highlights differences in group work orientation.

1. In working with a given group, I differentiate whenever possible between the aims of "guidance," "counseling," and "analytic therapy." I think of these as more or less unified, separate systems which frequently overlap. But too much blending results in confusion and wasted effort for my group and the agency.
2. I base my perceptions and understandings of process primarily on group dynamics principles (focus on studying the group as a unit) or on group therapy principles (focus on modifying a person's behavior within the group setting).
3. I am influenced by one or more schools of educational, psychological, or psychoanalytic thought; and I use this influence as my conceptual "set" as group leader.

On the other hand it is also helpful for the group worker to be aware of basic *similarities* between his group and other groups and between himself and other leaders. As the group counselor interacts with a culturally deprived group in a New York City junior high school, there are many similarities between his feelings of responsibility and commitment and those of a counselor-educator on the West Coast who is deeply involved in working with graduate students. In both examples group members are giving, receiving, expecting, and turning away in analogous ways.

The major common denominators among groups with varying aims and methods are observed by Murphy (1963, p.35). The author mentions three contributions of the group experience to the participant. They include: (1) the supply of "warmth and cohesion of a sort of family solidarity" and an opportunity to "become deeply identified with the other group members"; (2) the chance to develop "forms of social adaptation such as love and friendly competition"; (3) the possibility of "giving as well as receiving help."

Specifically, how can the group worker succeed in the transition from dialogue to group? Take the group counselor. He may readily examine already developed skills to see how they relate to his work in a group. A counselor who is familiar with the pre-drop-out apathy in an individual counselee seeks to use his insight in the group setting. In a high school counseling group, he asks Frieda to imagine the reactions of the others were she to leave school. Puzzled, the participants learn that Frieda, the "pre-drop-out," has a fantasy that several of the others are satisfied to have her fail. This is traced to her parents' wishes that she stay close to home. Frieda has always been dimly aware of how she is needed —if not used —to keep them together emotionally. Frieda is now able to see that in reality the group members are sorry about the prospect of her going and that, unlike the condition in her family, no one feels gratified about the prospects of her leaving. Through this interaction, Frieda has actually experienced some of the dynamics of her "dropping-out" problem.

At this point of training and experience, a counselor can take a fresh view of his place in a group. He sees that as a group leader he brings both facilitating and hindering influences. On the one hand, he may provide a model for asserting one's individuality without trampling on others, but on the other, he may carry the burden of feeling unable to do enough for his group. He may also wish to re-examine his skills in individual therapy, past group experiences, and commitments to the growth process in groups as he converts or adapts from individual to group.

The following five points refer to some of the strikingly different conditions which are met in groups. Mastery of these points is part of a leader's launching and maintaining the group as a rich experience for each of its members:

1. Recognizing the commonly stated or underlying resis-tances which group members have prior to and during the group experience;
2. Establishing viable ground rules — "the contract" — in keeping with the composition, setting, and goals of the

group;

3. Determining for himself what he can give and take in a group as leader-participant and understanding his own style of leadership and participation;

4. Employing his knowledge of roles (group-member, transactional, characterological, existential, or others) in the service of the individual, the group, and the theme;

5. Serving as the guardian of the group's interaction and life, especially in its early stages; screening for variety in membership; maintaining cohesiveness; keeping the ongoing process balanced by well-timed interventions.

Early Verbalized Resistances to Group

Whoever joins a group for a relatively brief but intensive experience — the "group process" situation (Berger, 1968) — is not likely to show the strong resistance usually expressed by one about to enter a therapeutic group. In this discussion we present a number of basic negative reactions by the participant noted prior to or during the group experience. We expect fewer advance signs of opposition from those in a "group process" group who seek knowledge about themselves or new experiences in one way or another. On the other hand a candidate for group therapy — voluntary or not — is often churning with anxiety and indecision about the new venture.

Resistances will be described under these headings: "Adherence to Formality — Invasion of Privacy," "Family Fears and Influences," "Dependence — Lack of Autonomy," "Difficulties with Emotional Expression and Control," and "Pretensions of Superiority."[1]

Adherence to Formality — Invasion of Privacy

One expressed resistance heard most often in schools and colleges is, "I don't feel comfortable about having different sets of relationships at school. As a 'student' I feel in place, but as a freely interacting group member I would be unable to shift gears, especially with a faculty member as leader. School is not the place to have my privacy invaded."

---

[1] I am indebted to Dr. Alexander Wolf who provided the basis for these formulations in a lecture, October, 1964.

It is most often a shy, inhibited student, safely concealed behind the formalities of school life, who raises questions about the suitability of school as a proper setting for his group experience. He could be assured that a group would provide a "safe" practice area for him and others who seek freedom to become more themselves. These additional points might appeal to this student's respect for intellectual achievement; if it is hard for him to convey ideas fully and creatively in class or with friends or if he is aiming for a profession which requires stronger blending of his emotional and thinking selves, group interaction would be the logical place to integrate these disjointed functions. He may also be reminded that while no one will force him to reveal private matters, he may do so after he hears others; indeed he will be likely to learn that what he has been keeping secret at great effort is revealed lightly by others in describing their own flaws.

Family Fears and Influences

The group member brings with him a tendency to experience the original family situation. Depending upon the genetic and analytic emphasis in the method employed, he becomes more or less aware of tendencies to react to others as siblings and parental figures. Certain objections made by beginning group members are traceable to an anticipated reliving of anxious feelings about early experiences in a family which had stifling, suppressive influences over its members.

Consider these common questions asked initially of a group leader: "Will I be able to leave if I don't like it?" "How can I be sure that confidentiality will be kept?" "Is it possible for strangers to talk freely about forbidden topics of sex, money, and aggression?" "What is done about scapegoating of members if indeed there is freedom of discussion and interaction?"

In response, the group leader emphasizes that in reality this is a far cry from an original family. Entrapment is not possible, since each person may come and go as he pleases. In addition, the group members are supportive of each other more often than might be expected. Finally, not withstanding that the others are now perceived as "outside strangers," the fearful participant may be assured that a friendly, cohesive spirit is frequently born at a very early stage.

Dependence — Lack of Autonomy

Another resistance is stated in a form which we may attribute in part to a lack of understanding about the workings of a group and in part to the dependent person's overestimating the leader. It is a common misconception — more so for therapy than process groups — that a person receives a fixed fraction of the attention from the leader as he would in an individual session. The candidate for a group who functions in a dependent way will seize upon the number of enrolled group members and question how much he can *get from the leader* in the presence of so many others. What he seems to be saying is, "I cannot function safely unless I am in possession of a stronger parent, teacher, friend, or marital partner." While no "instant therapy" can be performed to bring strength and daring to this group candidate, we can honestly tell him that if there are eight group members, there are in a sense eight therapists. We also inform him that the nominal leader readily takes a position in the circle along with other group members to encourage equality and independence.

Difficulties with Emotional Expression and Control

A distressing problem of our time is man's overcontrol or under-control of feelings, if indeed he is sufficiently in touch with feelings at all. The group experience is designed in good measure to re-capture these lost, strayed, or forgotten feelings. The prospective member, sensing that the best currency of honest interaction is *feeling,* worries about how he will function emotionally in the group. He wonders, "Will I win them over or will I be hurt by expressing feelings?" Or anxious about the implications of being controlled, he asks, "Will the group demand that I be spontaneous?"

With these questions and doubts, we see a reflection — appearing even more sharply in other cultures — of child-rearing practices aimed at reducing verbal and motoric emotional expression. We would raise a question with the group member-to-be about what he expects in return when he "puts his feelings on the line."

Does he feel vulnerable when there is no immediate positive response to his reaching out? Are words really that dangerous? And if the group members expect him to be spontaneous, are they forcing and controlling, or are they simply reaching out to feel his presence as a real person?

Pretensions of Superiority

An incoming group member may speak reluctantly of joining a group of people, commenting that they are more in need than he is. This resistance is recognizable in the form of flippant or contemptuous advance remarks about imagined other group members. Or perhaps he stresses an uncomplimentary report which he heard about what happened in another group. He feels he might be too advanced. Perhaps a group somewhere else would be more at "his level."

It is useful to question this person's defensively superior air directly by providing some important general facts (in this pre-induction stage) about the personal qualifications of other members. Can he see how this condescending attitude may have adversely affected other relationships? Does he not possess real assets without having to advance this objectionable "one upmanship?"

Additions to the Contract

"Contract" is defined as "an agreement between two or more parties for the doing or not doing of something specified." The contract in every planned group experience, we can say, has two parts: the *goals* of the service and the procedural *ground rules* for the "parties to the agreement."

Perhaps not enough attention is paid in the initial sessions to spelling out the provisions of the contract, briefly and informally. Child therapists are usually finely attuned to this situation. As an important contractual feature (partly illustrating goal and partly procedure), one therapist tells the boy or girl that he will try to get a clear picture of things "from the child's point of view," in effect declaring himself to be a species different from other more judgmental adults. In my child therapy training days at Childville, in New York, the basic agreement with the new patient not to break windows or attack the therapist bodily was formulated at the outset — even if only to protect life and limb.

In his discussion of contract, Menninger deals with the two elements formulated above. Regarding *goals,* he cites a range of patients' expectations, from learning to make better use of oneself in analysis to expecting a spontaneous cure through magical means. Regarding procedure, he asks the analysand to "experience the past and observe the present," (while the analyst is to "experience the present and observe the past").

If the contract in group sessions were to be glossed over, as often happens when a new member enters a "continuous group," confusion and misunderstanding of procedure and purpose could follow. A person who tends to feel anxious about asserting his presence (who in May's terms sits by quietly, never having learned to identify what he does fear and should fear) would need a stronger initial reminder about the agreement to share associations whenever possible.

Since the orchestration in a group is so complex at any given moment, the group leader might well avoid at least a gross pitfall by familiarizing himself with some general ground rules as well as those unique to specific groups. What follows are a number of guidelines useful to leaders, especially in the initial stages of a group. These "rules of the game" can be grouped into two areas: (1) confidentiality; (2) directives, ground rules, and guidelines.

Confidentiality

Although innocent or malicious gossiping or even threats of "extortion" would at first appear to be a hazard of the group experience, the fact is that there have been exceptionally few reports to this effect. Leakage occurs typically when a group member tells an outside intimate after the session about an event in the group involving himself. Another member may then be mentioned but not identified. However, even if seemingly aimless or compulsive talk about group occurs, the group ethos will make a person forego chancing injury to a fellow member and induce him to learn something for himself. The ensuing growth is often accompanied by feelings of mutual sharing and trust which have a built-in guarantee that confidences will be honored. Where the group meets for an intensive but brief period, the issue of confidentiality is further simplified.

While many leaders start off by insisting on using first names only, this practice is weakened when group members unavoidably and unguardedly identify themselves in other ways. Then, too, where the group meets in a small community or closed setting such as a school or agency, the pact of confidentiality is often put to a hard test. A college sophomore considering a group was vexed about "meeting other group members on campus." This anxiety was traced to her concern for confidentiality, for what she seemed to be saying was, "What will eight other people I meet daily do with my secrets?"

In brief, it is most effective for the group leader to state specifically that nothing shared by the participants should be repeated outside the group. If for some reason outside repetition does occur, the person is asked to bring it to the group meeting. Respect for privacy is an obligation just as binding on group members as it is on a counselor, analyst, lawyer, or clergyman in relationship to clients.

Directives, Ground Rules, Guidelines

Despite diverse schools of thought in counseling and psychotherapy, initial instructions given to the counselee have basic similarities. In addition to confidentiality, there are "house rules" about mode of interaction, attendance, cancellations, fees, and advance notice about leaving. Variations occur when the group leader (cognizant of his own special leanings, goals of members, and requirements of a particular setting) stresses such areas as problem-solving, unconscious material, interpersonal relationship, encountering, and nonverbal communication.

What follows are "staging" instructions for a T-Group and an analytic group. We present this material to illustrate the rich spectrum available to the group leader. First, the "group opening" described by Bradford (1964);

> "The trainer opened the group by stating that they would be together many hours during the laboratory session; that this provided an opportunity for each to increase learning and skill in knowing more about himself, in carrying out many of the functions expected of him in other situations, in being a more effective group member, in understanding group behavior; that these learnings could best be accomplished by analyzing whatever happened as they continued to meet together; and that he did not intend to serve as a group leader. He then stopped."

From the T-Group, stressing the desirable outcomes in learning about oneself and the life of the group, we turn to a representative first statement by practicing group therapists (Kadis et al., 1963);

> "Some therapists begin the opening session by simply stating that the group offers members an opportunity to talk about their feelings and eventually to understand their own patterns of behavior. It is not necessary for any person to feel compelled to reveal something he wants to keep to himself, but communicating freely is likely to help him gain understanding of his problems. Thus, the therapist can indicate his desire for the patients to bring up and discuss dreams, day dreams, fantasies, body sensations, and other unconscious material by merely asking, if no one brings any up spontaneously, 'Any dreams?' or 'You sit so tight'; or 'You clasped your hands so the knuckles are white.' Thus the group members can be helped to become aware of their body tensions and nonverbal expressions and the meaning of them."

In the preceding directive the group therapist encouraged the individuals to be free with their own communications, including those which are normally not revealed in usual verbal interchanges. Where the setting is *psychoanalysis in groups,* as described by Wolf and Schwartz (1960), there are a number of additional implied guidelines common to both group therapy and group psychoanalysis. While not spelled out in the initial contract with the group, the leader conveys this information to the group members at an early stage of their participation.

1. The equality of the group provides you with a greater opportunity for "positive relatedness" and "wholesome loving feelings."
2. Historical material is desirable and is crystallized easily for you by group interactions.
3. Your silences, far from being negative, "represent moments of restoration, integration, inner reflection or deep affect without the necessity to take action. . . ."
4. When the attention of the group is shifted away from you, it affords "a time to assimilate and work through, a time to help rather than be helped."
5. You will benefit by realizing that whatever you say will never result in your being destroyed. On the contrary,

reality proves that you may expect more support from the others than you imagine.

In the here-and-now experiential session described by Gendlin, there is still another emphasis. A series of eleven ground rules are directed toward members and leader alike. The "constitution" here is one of cooperative living; group belonging by right; emotional contact in depth; honesty of expression; group decisions that everyone favors. These are all considered to be the very fiber of effective participation in such a group.

The theme-centered interactional method has an important series of orientational guides of an existential purpose, described in Chapter VI. One of these instructions suggested by the leader at first feels jarring. It requires that the group member bring forth his distractions and disturbances whenever he feels that they interfere with his listening or contributing to the group. People are encouraged to declare at any point, "My mind is a blank" or "I feel so bored I'm drowsy" or "I cannot get my mind off the way Sally is leaning in her chair." The rationale for encouraging this seemingly disruptive behavior has an origin in the psychoanalytic priority of dealing first with resistance.

Styles of the Group Leader

For the leader, style, personality, and method are invariably interrelated. Of these factors, the developing leader probably finds that his personality blends style and method in one way or another. Where the individual counselor therapist, with personal difficulties may find some refuge in a passive or authoritarian manner, there is no place to hide in a group. One therapist who had personally achieved an enviable autonomy and self-assurance was highly successful in conducting group laboratories in which the participants learned a great deal about self-actualization. Another therapist who had mastered the intricacies of communication with her own marriage partner developed a natural, persuasive style of persistent, patient objectivity in communication which was translated effectively into specialized work with groups of married couples.

Although there are many examples of specific personality styles, the person entering group work may find it helpful to study three general orientations. While these were discussed by Hahn (1963) in the context of one-to-one relationships, the categories also illustrate group leaders' styles. The group worker may see himself doing something *to* the others, *for* the others, *with* the others, and (we may add) *along with* the others.

The so-called vertical[1] relationship describes the counselor-client affiliation where the one in need of help or advice looks up to the counselor as an expert, an authority. The more domineering, authoritarian counselor has this air. Here the group leader's "I" is obscured by dispensing, "expertising," giving to, and *doing something to* his subjects. An interesting example of this situation may be found in the very early writings on group treatment by Marsh (1931), who used the psychiatric ward as a setting. Using lectures, games, and even a final examination, Marsh drew from such sources as Rotary Club methods, Trudeau Sanitarium group method, methods of soul winning used by the Salvation Army, and, predominantly, the lecture-teaching model. Results reported by patients themselves were favorable. In this style it is "father who knows best."

Some group leaders are able to dispense with their fixed hierarchical position and encourage group members' autonomy. The group leader holds the reins not quite as tightly; he begins to acknowledge the influence of certain group member processes; he is doing things *for the others,* while maintaining a position at the apex of the triangle, with several group members in position at the base. Viewing the group as a family, we can identify this group leader more with the strong, generous parent who, recognizing groupings in the family, *does something for* the children, but on his or her own terms.

It takes a large measure of personal freedom and security, feelings of comfort in a group, and imaginativeness for the group leader to align himself "horizontally." He gives up the small luxuries of maintaining a professional air or of covering his own inadequacies. Relating authentically, with greater risk, and in Jourard's words "in the form of unself-conscious disclosure of self in words, decisions and actions," the leader *works with* the others. While giving up some of the benefits of the blank screen upon which a patient's

[1]Asya Kadis speaks of the "four different types of group communication": vertical, triangular, horizontal, and circular. We borrow these convenient terms to discuss varieties of leadership.

transferences are more clearly seen, this leader provides members with more opportunities for understanding their reality-based inter-actions with an authority. This style of leadership promotes progress in many other ways. Hostility may be more readily activated when the group member feels there will be less retaliation. Also the personal qualities of the leader — such as poise, objectivity, and honesty — when shared openly with the others facilitate growth-promoting identifications. With this style, the group leader does not relinquish his position as "the leader," or "counselor-therapist."

In some forms of group treatment and group experience, the leader occupies a "circular" position, in effect doing things *along with* the group. An early form of this approach at the individual level was Rosen's "direct therapy." Treating psychotic patients, the therapist let go of many ego defenses and "joined" the patient in regressive behavior. A current example of this style are those forms of "encounter" or "non-verbal communication" where the group leader joins the games, demonstrations, and microlabs as a full participant.

It would appear that working *along with* the group requires both the greatest and the least amount of talent, training, and personal qualifications in a leader. For on one hand, submerging oneself in the group could serve as a platform for the dependent, acting-out, exhi-bitionistic, countertransferring leader. On the other hand, it takes a mature, highly perceptive and unanxious leader to go so far out on stage, while remembering that he is still accountable for the quality of the real-life drama. One such leader with difficulty in resolving his own authority problems was present at a meeting of faculty leaders who were planning a "personal awareness" weekend for college students. Unable to agree on having just group leaders meet to ex-change experiences, even briefly, after each day's sessions, he com-plained, "Why not have students present at these meetings; they are generally just as sensitive as the leaders!"

The theme-centered interactional workshop leader frequently finds himself at various points along the scale. Momentarily, he be-comes "authoritarian" by enforcing a silence or by asking two people to enact a dialogue. But at the other end of the scale, he might relate to his "I" in a freely associative, self-revelatory way, virtually as a member of the group.

Roles of Group Members

The individual therapist recognizes at an early stage of his training that it is useful to experience or conceptualize about the patient in terms of patient-role. These manifestations are always observable and provide the therapist with global impressions about how the patient feels in therapy, such as "I am a helpless person seeking answers from you"; or "I am being exploited for the therapist's gain." The emerging roles are products of transferences, self-concepts, superimposed social attitudes, and factors related to age and development.

A recognition of roles can be helpful to the group leader who might otherwise become pinned down in a confusing barrage of seemingly unrelated events and reactions. Identification of these roles is useful — if not at times indispensable — in improving the quality and level of the group process. If each member has a share in nurturing the life and atmosphere of the ongoing group, his own role as a *group member* should be recognized and understood by leader and members. Benne (1964) classified member-roles into three broad groupings:

1. Group Task Roles, which include the initiator, information seeker, and orienter;
2. Group Building and Maintenance Roles, which include the encourager, compromiser, and follower;
3. Individual Roles, which include attempts by members to satisfy individual needs for aggression, blocking, recognition, and seeking help.

The individual-oriented group analyst or one who stresses encounter in leading a group might readily discount the value of dealing with "group roles" for other than research purposes. Yet it is difficult to imagine how any group leader does not in some way relate intuitively to this "on stage" behavior of the participants. There are still many other ways of characterizing the group member, such as in his degree of helpfulness to others, character of resistance, tendency toward inhibition, somaticized anxiety, or various characterological designations.

With the proliferation of group approaches (as with the theme-centered interactional workshop method) it is still too early to define those group task roles and individual roles which promote maximum growth and progress. Yet in a general way we can recall the best results when there has been a balance among the following dialectical pairs of approaches to group membership: autonomy and interdependence, pre-established goals and new-found ones, insight and action, egotistic and socially responsible expression of feeling, reality and fantasy, fragmentation and reconstruction.

Life and Vitality of the Group

The ill effects of technological and dehumanizing influences in our society have encouraged the counterforce of rebuilding human and group potential. More than ever before, the self needs healing and revitalizing; communities demand redesigning and reconstructing. Group work has responded in two new directions: One is the tremendous interest in the human growth experience by way of sensory, perceptual, and emotional development. The second is the friendly invasion of the "new" group work by those who seek to solve urban, religious, political, and educational problems through group "power." Understandably, such enthusiastic steps in the face of desperate social pressures have taken attention away from time-consuming, tedious, and disciplined study of ongoing group process. Yet whether the leader is identified with a specific system and profession or whether there is a looser or paraprofessional attitude, the life and vitality of the group is nourished by the leader's conceptual and emotional grasp of group phenomena.

Already mentioned are the doubts and criticisms which a group member can present even prior to entering the group. These objections are best brought to light by the group leader before or during the initial sessions so as to neutralize the destructive effects upon the individual and group. If these early resistances are overcome, there is yet another challenge which affects the very existence of the group. Here we refer to those group dynamics or processes which serve to keep the mood or atmosphere either vibrant and alive or stiff and formalistic. Three important features of an alive and well group are: (1) cohesiveness and balance; (2) "fit" of the individuals' capacities and goals to the overall process and structure of the group; and (3) effectiveness of the leader in contacting individuals, fostering authentic interaction, balancing the ongoing events, and dealing with group resistances.

The cohesive and varied group moves along with parts generally well oiled. Giving the spirit a voice: "We are here together; I feel connected with what's going on; I am gaining from this experience." A positive tone is fed by reciprocal acceptance, a relaxed but expectant mood, and a feeling of common purpose. The members have accepted some of the implicit social values of the group. They include seeing others as different but equal, and using the group to facilitate growth and learning through openly examining oneself and others. There is a balance between readiness to reveal scars of one's own experience and to treat the wounds of others in a healing way.

For a varying group composition, no specific formula is available. Certainly, glaring discrepancies in age, intelligence level, cultural background, and male-female ratio tend to create a Tower of Babel effect — unless this kind of heterogeneity is built in as part of the design, interracial, interreligious, and family groups are examples. A balance of personality types is considered important, particularly in smaller groups where random sampling would not take effect. Consider the impact of an entire group of eight talkative, competitive, aggressive people. Who would listen? In elementary schools especially, children at these ages tend to cling to peer group identifications and would find it rather distracting to be with those above or below their grade level.

Matching the Individual with the Group

In the recent group explosion enthusiasm has run so high that a careful look at any one of the ubiquitous groups in operation would reveal unfortunately that individuals and their groups do not always "fit." In one college week-end human potential group, there were several shy, inarticulate students who were there to find a way out of their loneliness. Actually there were several potent interpersonal reactions, with resulting release and insight for some students. For the shy ones, however, the bridge between this intense experience and their everyday lives was missing. In fact, they were already quite sensitive to nonverbal signals but needed a way of channeling these intuitions into making and keeping friends. A general criticism cited for loosely run sensitivity experiences is that the tendency to use forced interactions and to dredge up pathology makes these experiences unfit for many of the participants.

This problem of *"fit"* is as challenging in therapeutic as in experiential groups. A patient who needed direction and structure because of the lack of firm parents had a faulty experience in group therapy with a well-trained existential analyst. The therapist had relinquished leading and directing in favor of exclusively relating as another member of the group.

Another poor "fit" in terms of the counselee's general readiness for a group experience can occur in school counseling services when the intake procedure improperly evaluates the student's ability to observe himself and others in the presence of others. Under pressures of scheduling, availability of group counselors, demands of referring sources, and other exigencies, the student may be placed immediately in a group without the necessary "training" in individual sessions. The suitability of a given group for a specific counselor on the other hand may be enhanced by the relatively undeveloped and unexplored "combined counseling" plan wherein group and individual sessions are provided concurrently.

The Leader in Action

The degree and quality of the leader-participant contact is crucial for building a sense of belonging and encouraging members to risk the unknown. In this sense the leader is a gracious host, a provider. But unlike the house visitor who need not stay or return, the group member sojourns not as a "guest" but simply as himself. Insufficient contacts between leader and participants can lead to the latter feeling neglected, followed by tendencies to ignore the leader in turn or to waste efforts in attracting attention.

Contact has to be renewed frequently by glance, touch, word, or other means which assure the participant of the leader's understanding and commitment. The beginning group leader can develop such empathy by an awareness of various kinds of manifest connections between the individual and group. If there is holding back, disappointment, self-consciousness, frustration — or any one of many individual-to-group feelings — the skilled leader relates to each member by acknowledging and respecting these feelings.

Balancing in a group provides variety, challenge, and possibilities for growth. The "balance of nature" or "well-balanced diet" applied to group work refers to the encouragement of a variety of processes which contribute not only toward the goals of the individual in his becoming autonomous and interdependent but also toward the goal of the group as a whole in its establishing a cohesive spirit. The effective leader, without becoming controlling or obtrusive, balances the bewildering assortment of phenomena which emerges in any one session.

A creative approach to these balances and imbalances will guide the individual practitioner in making a transition to groups. A group can suffer from too much focus on the "I" or on the "we"; from the droning of intellectualization or the waves of emotion; from preoccupation with root causes or the heady texture of the existential moment; from a research orientation by the leader or an activist no-theory-at-all view; from too much spurious loving or too much spurious hating. Even though group members learn to sense and effectively call attention to these skewed situations, the leader bears chief responsibility to intervene for the sake of proportion and balance, at least in the initial sessions.

Group resistance which emerges from a build-up of unexpressed individual distractions and covert disagreements with the group experience can sap the life and vitality of the group. Group members typically have real or transferential interferences with becoming fully engaged with the leader, the other members, or the stated goals of the group. In individual psychoanalysis, resistance is expected, used, and worked through. But in groups the resistive alliance readily takes the form of a counter group work force which is spent in "putting down" the leader and the contract. In classrooms where the teacher, school, or "system" has lost the respect of the pupils, a form of group resistance results. Individuals and subgroups ignore or harass the leader; there is destructive acting out in or outside the group; and people are absent or come late. In the following illustration one frightened, resistive group member galvanized others into expressing distrust, defensiveness, and hostility toward the leader who symbolized an oppressive authority. This group had a history of discord among its members.

A number of teachers were consulting with a counselor about improving group dynamics skills. One teacher, unable to tolerate references to ongoing, here-and-now group process, "refused to have group therapy." Instead he wanted to talk about classroom experiences. He persistently accused the leader of using "techniques" (thereby denying the very basis of and contract for the meeting). He further challenged the leader's authority by defending several participants whom he thought were "unfairly" called on for "personal" feelings about their work. Others, disgruntled with the unfairness in their working arrangements, displaced their hostility about the system onto the consultant whose slightly formal air gave surface credence that the consultation was secretly imposed and authoritarian. After several sessions of this kind, the consultant decided with the group that no further progress was possible. The group was disbanded.

This was not to be the time or place — or group — for dissolving such massive resistances. In TCI terms, since there was such contamination of the I-We-It functioning, the leader withdrew wisely and strategically, admitting to a momentary but not lifelong defeat.

2

A
TCI
Workshop
Model

VI

Map
and
Territory

Introduction

In previous chapters we have used outline tables to remind the reader of the range of known group procedures. Some orientation about the TCI method has been provided throughout. We now continue our study of the TCI method in greater depth in a structured review of its main features and terrain. Features of the method will be stated briefly, then amplified.

In several case illustrations to follow, we are using a transcript of a workshop with seven male and female high school students, sophomores and juniors. Of mixed races and religions, they were all "advantaged" with the exception of one Puerto Rican boy. They volunteered to attend five two-hour sessions after school every week on the subject of personal communication, announced by the principal. The "Urban Prep School" is college oriented, of high standards, with rich programs and a lively, friendly atmosphere. Both co-leaders were from outside the school. The theme, "My Participating and Alienating," was announced by the leaders at the first session. "Leader R" was Ruth C. Cohn. "Leader M" was Myron Gordon.

Detailed Features of TCI

1. Definition

An experiential method (integrating educational, group-dynamic, and therapeutic features) which may be adapted to group needs, problem solving, and a variety of themes.

Ruth C. Cohn (1970) offers a detailed definition of the structural factors of the theme-centered interactional method as follows:

Group interaction is graphically described as a "triangle in the globe." The triangular points designate the functions of the individual (I), the group (We), and the theme (It). The *I* comprises the awareness and activity of the individual in the interaction with the group; the *We* designates the concern of each person for all others and the theme; the *It* is the purpose for which the group convenes. The globe is the time-space and other givens of the environment — school, organization, community, country, the network of purpose, and motivation of the outside-of-the-group population. The inside group interaction is co-determined by the globe; thus the TCI group brings values and influences of the university, town, parents, and political-historical situations into the group interaction.

The theme is defined as the focus of interaction. It marks the group's existence as a cohesive entity and not a crowd (subway riders, cocktail party). The theme must be of interest to all group participants, or else cohesion cannot come to pass. Establishing a theme as a common denominator is the basis for group interaction (counseling themes may be "Achieving Better Communication," "Being Myself with Others," "Toward Finding Ways to Study Productively," "Being a Sexual Partner," etc.).

The individual is as important as the group, the group as important as the individual. In this world of mass depersonalization the individual's need to find his identity is paramount. Only when people respect their uniqueness and accept their living-learning potential can they find a place in this world and be effectual partners within small groups and large communities.

Belonging to one world, people cannot find their identity without accepting partnership. This paradox of finding individuality only through partnership is universal. The process of groups augments the opportunities for both intrapersonal and interpersonal effectiveness. The group's need for cohesion around the theme carries a power to help the individual with his various strivings to focus in the direction of the stated purpose.

The TCI method may be further defined in terms of its greater elasticity than group therapy, teaching, or everyday conversation. In TCI there is a maximum degree of candor which can be accommodated or risked. At the same time there is the added feature of resilience, how neatly the interactions can be encouraged to bounce back to the theme. In therapy groups the trend to candor can become rigid when candor becomes an end in itself; in education groups a constricting factor is that the adherence to purpose may limit the freedom of the leader, the group, and its members; in normal conversation a tightening and an avoidance of true feelings can take place as an effect of overconcern with how others regard us.

2. *Theoretical Basis*

The "I" is best shaped and released when the interactions are focused around a theme.

A concise statement of theoretical bases and assumptions by Cohn covers three areas:

1. The philosophy of this method is basically humanistic. We are psychological beings, reactive and active as (autonomous) entities; we are also partners of society and the conditions of the universe and thus interdependent. Our autonomy and interdependence require that we make choices within the framework of societal and earthly givens. Awareness of autonomy and interdependence promotes the growth of individuals and groups.

2. Authentic communication between educator and student bridges gaps from person to person and from group to group. A teacher, priest, or counselor cannot tell a student which choices to make, but he can aid him by exposing to him his vision of the world and his own experiences and credo — avoiding both pseudo-neutrality and authoritarian omnipotence.

3. Groups are people who come together for the sake of a common purpose, which may range from personal encounter to worldly tasks. In any communicative enterprise or educational situation, all members of a group are as effective in their cooperation as their motivations and skills will allow them to be.

In theory, these principles are maintained by participants through the use of releasers and shapers. Releasers have to do with stoking the energy of a participant (example: asking the group members to speak for "I"). Shapers relate to making the process produce interactional growth and learning (example: centering the theme and encouraging associations of all kinds in giving to and accepting from the theme).

3. Referral

By self or through response to announcement.

The versatility of this method makes possible a very wide range of referral. The chief criterion for referral and acceptance to a TCI group is the person's interest in pursuing a given theme with others over a specific period of time. Because of the cohesive and accepting mood which is encouraged, we do not anticipate flare-ups of hidden pathology. On the contrary, each participant is encouraged to reach the true range of his competence in the context of pursuing a task. When a person at any age, in any locale, for any reason does not seek out help for a painful life — yet searches for a better life — a referral to a TCI group would be in order.

4. Aims — Benefits

To release spontaneity while maintaining responsible focus on a theme. Result: more effective use of energy for learning.

The implied aim may be stated in more universal terms: we strive to balance the person in thought, feeling, expression, and movement — the TCI model of man. Our frequent use of the word "workshop" also conveys another implied aim. We wish to acknowledge the social nature of knowledge, the social nature of work, and the meaning of life given by accomplishment. For these reasons we foster a group method which brings people together not simply for an emotional or intellectual encounter but for an actual life task in which content, process, and self are combined.

In the following excerpts from the "Urban Prep School" tape, both leaders converge on Don who frequently "tuned out" despite obvious interest and liveliness before and after the actual group meetings. Energy which was locked in boredom was blocked in the group. The group leaders sought to light some sparks by bringing Don into closer contact with his inner feelings and his interpersonal needs while keeping the theme in focus.

Leader R (to Don): Are you bored? The rule is you must interrupt.

Don: I'm bored (others laugh).

Leader R: You feel alienated because you are bored.

Don (to Ed): I know you are bored too.

Ed: I'm not bored.

Leader M (to Don): I remember you told about how you

would like to "boom out" in this group.

Don: I just don't feel so involved.

Leader R: The question is what do you do about being bored; you are alienated. Now what would you have to do, or what would have to happen by others, to make you less bored.

Don: No matter what we're talking about . . . the others . . .

Leader R: Never mind the others. You have the obligation of not being bored. We'll talk about being bored. If you talk about being bored, you'll be involved.

5. Duration and Composition

From 3 to 100 hours in short-term, intensive, day-long or week-end sessions; or weekly over one year. From six to twenty in a group.

Lending itself to a variety of situations, the TCI group serves well even where there are contrasts among members and subgroups. The method is designed to encourage each person to approach the theme in his own way. Thus some kindergarten children, a supervisor, a teacher, a parent, and a few fifth grader "aides" could all prosper in the same TCI group with the theme of "Learning About Myself and Others with Finger Paints." Faculty members who teach different subjects, adults and adolescents, paraprofessionals and teachers and many others of clashing interests and personalities find themselves communicating better than before. This situation seems to evolve because the TCI group has the machinery for working through the actual antagonisms between and contradictions among people — antagonisms which would otherwise keep them from getting to the "nitty gritty" of what their rational relationship could be within the context of their living or working with others in the group.

6. Ground Rules

Cohn (1969) has expressed TCI ground rules with great clarity:
 — Be your own chairman. Decide what you want to

do.
— Give to this situation what you want to give to and get from it.
— Disturbances and passionate involvements take precedence over the stated theme in order to be re-solved.
— Speak for I and not for We.
— Make as many statements as possible and ask only important questions.

At first glance these rules are deceptively simple. Some group workers after hearing these five statements have questioned their importance and effect. In fact, if most of these simple precepts were used indiscriminately outside of intimate groups, chaos, rejection, or embarrassment could easily follow. Imagine a committee meeting on drug abuse in your school, with several visiting assistant principals present. Your principal is chairman. Could you follow the first ground rule to "be your own chairman," to say that you regret some of the neglected features of drug prevention in your school? Only in a humanistically advanced society or in the safety of a TCI or other group can you safely bring into personal awareness and interplay the neglected side of the self as you are acting and interacting more freely.

The ground rules are designed basically to promote autonomous and interdependent functioning. They are geared to encourage the development of consciousness together with awareness. If, for example, you ask many questions, you cannot become conscious of the feelings, attitudes, and values you have, since they are being successfully masked by the act of questioning another. Another important function of the ground rules is to open the gates for releasing locked-up energy. The analyst asks the patient to free him-self by saying whatever comes to mind. The TCI leader has found a way to encourage the same in a living-learning situation by encour-aging the airing of any distractions from the theme. (See further details in Chapter XII.) Another way of releasing energy is the abolition of the word "we" (when a group member is generalizing about others in the group). If a member represents the "others'" point of view, he is usually taking on a role or making a judgment which completely obscures his own real feelings by avoiding the use of "I."

In these excerpts from a fourth session at the Urban Prep

School, group members began by talking noisily with each other, disregarding the leaders. This "uncooperative" group was fully engaged in discussing a recent humorous school event involving boys fighting in a classroom. A variety of interventions were made by the leaders in efforts to deal with what was becoming a massive distraction. By referring to, acting on, and clarifying some of the ground rules, the leaders were able to get back the attention of the group of adolescents, several of whom had alienated the "adult" TCI leaders.

Leader R: When I came in, I felt like a girl of twelve with a much older group.

Vic: Because you came late, you weren't with it!

Leader R: What's going on now is *no* authority, *no* rules. (Group disregards this, following by joking with sexual overtones.)

Leader R: The only authority is the rule about "being your own chairman," and you are rebelling against your own authority.

Marion: You said "interrupting" is all right.

Leader M: But not just "butting in." Interrupting can be of value if the person decides that his giving or getting at that point is really important. (Group members continue to talk all at once about the play *Hair*.)

Leader R (acting on her own feeling of alienation from the group): I'd like to know what you say about the group when you are not here.

Trudy: We don't talk about it.

Leader R (cutting through this quick rebuff): What *would* you say if you did?

Vic (in a dissatisfied tone): Alienating is participating, and participating is alienating.

Leader M (to Vic): I have low tolerance for feeling insulted, and what you said makes it seem to me that the work and planning I did is being degraded.

Terry: We should feel insulted too because we put in just as much time as you.

Leader R (to Terry): [Leader M] has just as much a right to his feelings as anyone else.

Frank: I sympathize with [Leader M]. What is important to him, Vic breaks down.

Leader R (summarizing and articulating while still touching the theme): If I want to participate, either I adjust to the others or the others adjust to me.

7. Content

Exploration and fulfillment of the theme.

While the TCI approach is markedly person centered and experiential, an extremely wide range of content may be introduced. (Chapter IX is devoted to themes.) The Fall 1968-1969 bulletin of the Workshop Institute for Living-Learning lists the following offerings: (for professionals) "Recent Advances in Sexual Knowledge and Implications for Psychotherapy"; (for WILL staff) "Here-and-Now-and-Next in our Community Work"; (for leaders in community programs) "Group Teaching and Group Process"; (for interested people) "Body Awareness," "The Challenge of Being Me," "America's Problem and I," "Violence in our World — in Me, in You, in our Children."

Through the format of the TCI group we travel with participants far and wide, through id, ego, and superego, from human values in a playground to organizational matters in a large company. In Chapter XII we propose that the theme be therapy. The range of content and theme is limited only to what goes on with and within people.

8. Special Nature of Experience and Uniqueness

Increased modes of being oneself emerge and the relationship between them can be worked out and explained.

One-to-one relating takes place in the context of a number of people becoming a group in the light and warmth of a theme.

At the heart of the TCI method are three series of characteristics which support its special and unique nature:

a. *Flexibility, openness, spontaneity, and prudence.* Integrations and adaptations from other techniques are easily absorbed. Thus, for example, encountering may be used, but in the framework of rational understanding. Teaching has its place, but it takes a humanistic form. Counseling may be employed, but it is focused on the themes being explored.

b. *More effective energy release.* The individual is opened up and encouraged to take chances. Fragmented images of the self are elicited and shared, since no one is expected to come in with work already done. Emphasis is thus on the stripping bare of emergent dilemmas rather than on the less dynamic remembrances of problems past.

c. *Built-in living-learning, making one's life an act of living itself.* This goal is accomplished through "dynamic balancing" and "centering." It refers to the formations of the most practical and aesthetic relationship at a given time for the individual between the I, We, and It; between himself, environment, and thought; between emotion, practical involvement, and knowledge.

This excerpt was taken from a college course of twenty men and women in which the TCI method was employed, using a succession of themes on the college student, learning, and personal growth. In this third session, the theme was "My Learning — Alive or Dead." Illustrated here are the free-flowing comments of a number of students about their educational experiences at college. George's remark at the end will be discussed as an illustration of "centering" or "dynamic balancing."

Ron: In science, memorization and regurgitation of facts is dead learning.

Myra: There were some things you *did* like.

Leader A (to Myra): What about *your* interest in science?

Myra: I always took courses I liked. I liked psych reading but would have liked more field work.

Evie: It isn't that theory is dead and practice alive. It's using what I have to grow.

Leader A (to Evie): Do you have a concrete example?

Evie: I was stimulated enough in high school to go on with French and music myself.

James: One experience in which I grew was a high school physics course where you worked independently.

Leader B (to James): It's exciting that you had such a curiosity to find out about how electricity worked.

James: I was fascinated by what caused it.

George: I did something like that in an Honors Program.

Leader B (to James): I'm still thinking of a quality you have which can make you fascinated by things.

James: Yes, it's there, but I hold myself back a lot. You can become *afraid* to uncover what you like.

Myra: One teacher lectured over our heads, but we were afraid to tell him we didn't understand the lecture.

Leader A: I know I can't keep in touch even with twenty students in a course.

George: People are not interested here. What are we doing about a viable alternative in education? Nothing can come of this discussion unless I go to the Dean of Faculty.

Leader A (to George): This *is* a practical situation here.

Ron: Trouble is, everyone is expecting a miraculous effect here. But if you try so hard, you won't get anything.

Myra: I have no expectations. I'm interested in other

people, what I can contribute to them. I'd be satisfied just
for that.

George: Maybe I'm selfish — I want to get more than
participating.

The events preceding George's last remark serve as a backdrop.
George, an active, forceful student leader, had become impatient
with the lack of practical, expediting solutions by others. He had
confided to one of the leaders in the beginning of the course that
what he lacked in his college years was an awareness of how others
saw him. As others gave more and more of their personal reactions,
he began to see the discrepancy between his style of getting things
done, committee work and political maneuvering, and the various
revelations of how feelings could influence living and learning.
George's comment at the end was a form of "centering." He
referred to his feeling at that moment as "selfish" (the I). He was
addressing his comment to the group as a whole as if to make contact with them from a real and felt part of himself (bringing in the
We). His thought or task (the It) was that he wanted to get more out
of group learning than "participating." He seemed to be searching
for another concept of participation to exchange for the barren,
efficient one to which he had always been accustomed.

9. Stages — Sequences

(1) Setting constructive climate; beginning focus on theme
and interaction; (2) dynamic development of the theme,
interactions, and intrapsychic events; (3) termination and
resolution of group interaction; continuation of individual's
development outside the group.

The experienced worker or practitioner in any field can readily
conceptualize three stages of a task: first, middle, and last. When
you start, be sure first to set the stage, create the right conditions,
and evaluate what you are working with and what you have to do.
The middle phase is the body of the task or assignment. Work on,
work out, work through the building process of the job. Finally, upon
completion, separate from the finished product, and carry on with
the effects of the accomplishment.

At the inception of the initial phase, the leader's responsibility is
at its highest. The setting, the purpose, the preferred pathways, and

the group composition have all been carefully taken into account. The first plunge, or "opening in three steps," is characteristic of TCI workshops. This is an overture which embodies in itself the elements which make up the interaction and focused life of the ensuing group process. The three steps, separated by a minute or two of silence, are 1) cognitive, 2) affective, 3) dramatic.

> Step 1) The leader asks everyone (including himself) to close his eyes and picture himself involved in some work; to let himself clearly see the task to be done and the way of carrying it through.

> Step 2) The leader again asks the members to become aware of how they feel now in this group with these people and with the theme.

> Step 3) The leader asks everyone to open his eyes and choose one person who might hamper or stifle his work; then choose one person who it is surely felt will enhance his ingenuity in work.

This three-step opening calls forth the group machinery and individual energies which together serve as a springboard and context for functioning in a theme-centered way.

10. Leader

> While embodying the functions of a self-actualizing member, he acts as the regulator of the I (self), We (group interaction), and It (theme).

The leader must take the initiative — especially at first — to insure a cohesive, accepting atmosphere. To this end, he must sense the hopes, expectations and dreams radiating from each beginning group experience. But where the momentum of group movement in working out themes or tasks is weighed against the preservation of individual integrity, the leader will allow some loss of the former in deference to the latter.

Beyond this task, in common with the best of teaching and therapy practice, the leader is persistently mindful of the people he is working with rather than preoccupied with achievement of the group's or leader's goals. He cultivates each member's pace of participation and growth with respect for individual differences. While he is enthusiastic about how much productive interaction well-running groups can accomplish, he maintains guardianship of the individual's right to air disturbances and question the main trend. This receptivity for the feelings and comments of group members extends itself even to hostility expressed by individuals.

As a "model participant" he leads by example in observing the ground rules of the TCI method. Besides serving as a balance for process, the leader gauges and encourages the connections which the participants are making between themselves and the theme.

The workshop leader more often than not is confronted with the deeper pathology of some group members whose intentions were to engage in an active and positive way. But in the vicissitudes of group life, their pathology breaks through their defenses and becomes evident to the leader and possibly to other participants —if not to themselves. This is the time for the leader's tactful guidance, supportive attitudes and acceptance, rather than full-blown therapy.

Cohn's graceful remark about the TCI leader is:

"The group leader of a TCI group invariably goes through periods of peace and periods of disturbance. There is a disquietude in holding the responsibility for the balance between personal and work concerns. When do I interrupt? When do I just gently shift communications by expressing myself with my own feelings or thoughts? How does the leader deal with a growing distraction from the theme, such as the centering of attention on one personality trait of a group member, beyond any connection with the theme? Calling attention to the process (in this case the group member's reluctance to state that he really wanted the therapeutic investigation stopped) resulted in a shift back to the theme."

These excerpts from the Urban Prep School group will further illuminate the leader's work both in serving as a model of authenticity and in providing balances between content and process.

Leader R (early in first session during a silence, leader attempts by example to bring forth honest, authentic interactions): I feel apprehension about whether this will work out.

Terry: What is the age range here? (Several people give their ages.)

Vic (implying that as a minority member he is trapped by society): Alienation results from society's definition that you are different. When I was a little kid, I was excluded from certain "in-groups." From seventh grade on, I didn't mind.

Leader R (a double-barrelled comment referring to both cognitive data and the immediate): They did something to you . . . because you were different. I don't know if he alienates himself or is alienated by others. . . . Now he is alienating himself.

Vic (responding to the leader's interest in him, he reveals more about himself): I had feelings about dating for a long time . . . making the right impression.

Leader M (continuing to bring in the present, but with an interactional emphasis): How does it feel, Shelley, to be the only girl here now?

Shelley (glancing at the door): I wish the others would get here.

Leader R (sensing the divisive tendency toward forming subgroups in response to a new situation): Could we sit a little closer?

(Chairs are pushed closer. Group members look more intently at each other.)

The leaders have been fully employed observing the ongoing verbalizations and nonverbal actions. Group leader M later recalled how his own feelings of warmth about such young people with "the guts" to join an unknown experience almost prompted him to reveal more about himself than may have been appropriate in this first session. Leader R was aware of her following the idea of Vic's inducing more alienation than was actually present, thereby compounding the problem and also making it difficult for Vic to deal integratively and productively with the problem others were forcing on him.

11. Member

Defers to the positive tone the workshop fosters; lets the relationships develop in the course of making the theme his reality.

Each person can use the time to be himself through the whole range of human possibility. He is encouraged to respond and encounter but not to censure or invoke conformity, no matter how subtle.

The member serves as his own learner, teacher, "therapist," leader, and chairman while others around are invited to do the same interdependently. We have frequently observed one of the most common ways to cloak oneself unknowingly, avoiding the word "I": "We don't know what your purpose is with this group," or "The boys in this group would prefer sitting on the floor," are classical examples of unsuccessful efforts by the participant to make a self-statement. As the members receive frequent reminders to speak for themselves, they begin to see others emerging clearly and colorfully while the haze of the mystical "group we" happily disappears.

12. Motivation — Resistance

Motivation is heightened by the natural excitement of manifold possibilities for learning. Resistance takes the form of being too I, We, or It centered or of distractions away from the theme.

Members perceive TCI as a useful medium for learning and behavioral change accompanied by the pleasure of a social experience. All of these are built right into the fabric of the group experience.

A unique yet commonly observed resistance appears in TCI groups. In this form a member complains that there is something wrong with the *process.* He recalls that when he was once in a sensitivity group, they played games which got everybody involved with each other more rapidly instead of sitting around guardedly. Another person (in the same group!) complains of the absence of "hard content." Still another fellow member is indignant about the leader announcing guidelines "so authoritatively." As TCI is characterized by shifting processes, the participants engage in a new "resistance," in the guise of a plausible complaint about an overemphasis on the I, We, It, or leader's role. The resistance is often based on the participant's reluctance and difficulty in bringing forth less accessible features of his own functioning which would make for richer living-learning.

13. Transferences — Realities

Transference is minimized as the syntaxic mode is favored with respect to the theme, the others, the leader, and the self.

The leader confronts transference illusions — whenever possible — with present persons and present events. Cohn has described some criticisms and signs of admiration which, while having possibilities for transferential analysis, are responded to by the TCI leader more in the light of reality. These criticizing and praising comments go like this: "Why did you lecture so much in this last session (for three minutes!) rather than let the interaction flow? Why did you not lecture more — it was time for clarification! Why did you not create a firmer structure — how could one get anywhere with all these interferences? How did you achieve the kind of perceptivity to be geared to everybody and the theme at the same time?"

The TCI leader with background and experience in psycho-dynamics will at times erroneously lean toward the transferential. When this shift happens, the member is taken by surprise and will experience some discomfort and confusion. In an education methods course, the TCI leader had a discussion on the effects of some sample small-group projects with the college class members as participants. An older member with tense and angry expression declared that the discussion was doing no good and that it had cut short the time of the small-group activity. The TCI leader commented about her impatience and was told that this student had waited for "many years" to complete her training as a teacher. The leader then stated that the student seemed to be blocked by the leader. This remark was turned down by the student who after class told the leader that she didn't want these feelings discussed in the presence of others. A less transferential remark by the leader could have been, "I do not mean to be holding up your education; I have scheduled this group discussion to enable you to train yourself as a professional teacher with a knowledge of every aspect, etc.''

In the following table, the main features of the TCI workshop model are listed serially, according to their appearance in this chapter.

TABLE 11
Theme-Centered Interactional Workshop

1. *Definition*	An experiential method (integrating educational, group-dynamic, and therapeutic features) which may be adapted to group needs, problem-solving, and a variety of themes.
2. *Theoretical Basis*	The "I" is best shaped and released when the interactions are focused around a theme.
3. *Referral*	By self or through response to announcement.
4. *Aims — Benefits*	To release spontaneity while maintaining responsible focus on a theme. Result: more effective use of energy for learning.
5. *Duration and Composition*	From 3 to 100 hours in short-term, intensive, day-long or week-end sessions; or weekly over one year. From six to twenty in a group.
6. *Ground Rules*	Promoting autonomous and interdependent functioning and aiming at consciousness together with awareness. (See section on ground rules, Chapter VI.)
7. *Content*	Exploration and fulfillment of the theme.
8. *Special Nature of Experience and Uniqueness*	Increased modes of being oneself emerge and the relationship between them can be worked out and explained. One-to-one relating takes place

in the context of a number of people becoming a group in the light and warmth of a theme.

9. *Stages — Sequences*

(1) Setting constructive climate; beginning focus on theme and inter-action; (2) dynamic development of the theme, interactions, and intra-psychic events; (3) termination and resolution of group interaction, continuation of individual's development outside the group.

10. *Leader*

While embodying the functions of a self-actualizing member, he acts as the regulator of the I (self), We (group interaction), and It (theme).

11. *Member*

Defers to the positive tone the workshop fosters; lets the relationships develop in the course of making the theme his reality.

12. *Motivation — Resistance*

Motivation is heightened by the natural excitement of manifold possibilities for learning. Resistance takes the form of being too I, We, or It centered or of distractions away from the theme.

13. *Transferences — Realities*

Transference is minimized as the syntaxic mode is favored with respect to the theme, the others, the leader, and the self.

VII

A
TCI
Group
in
Action

We now wish to convey the actual style, spirit, and workings of a TCI group. A four-hour workshop (consisting of one session) is selected as an illustration. We call it the Galveston Group. This is a voluntary adult group consisting of ten male and female teachers and community mental health workers who enrolled for a workshop entitled "Autonomy and Interdependence." While the content is unusual for its high level of verbal intelligence, the process is comparable with that of other age groups. The tape is selected not only as a model of effective TCI leadership but also for its variety of TCI processes.

First we provide a summary of the main event of the workshop

— a sequence of "still shots" with captions — and explain them in TCI terms. Evidence of TCI principles, structures, and procedures are developed. Following this is a small slice, covering one fifth of the actual protocol, along with detailed interpretations of ongoing process and comments on content.

Main Flow of the Galveston Group

The main flow of events in the Galveston Group will be portrayed, followed intermittently by focus on principles, procedures, and structures of the TCI method — wherever they may seem to apply.

Episodes and Comments: Opening

1. Leader opens with theme and invites introspection with three silences.

This is a typical and ingenious opening which requires modification for each new workshop according to theme, members, and setting. The leader announces the theme and asks for *silent* thought about its meaning to bring members cognitively closer to the theme. To initiate interactive attitudes, the leader asks for a second silent period, inviting the participants to become aware of their inner feelings and sensations in the here and now. Then calling for a third silent task, the leader asks for brief eye contacts around the room. This particular exercise was designed to connect the theme actively to an ongoing, specific activity.

Episodes and Comments : Initial Phase

2. Members attempt to define the theme, personally and in cognitive terms.

3. Members interact around the distrust of "interdependence" related to the incident of a carelessly used tape in a school.

4. Leader focuses on Alice's distrust of interdependence.

5. Leader continues focus on highlighting the individual; an encouragement to deal more with the "I," e.g., Blanche's

heartbeat. Blanche tries to evaluate her own "crazy" type of autonomy.

6. Leader differentiates autonomy from autism.

7. Charles brings in his personal experience with autonomy where he objected to racial prejudice.

8. Members explore the theme rationally.

This sequence bring us through the initial stage, about one fifth of the total time. The leader has concentrated on establishing a constructive climate in several ways: (1) she herself has been a participant by freely relating her own thoughts and feelings about the theme; (2) she has emphasized the positive elements of whatever is being said; (3) she has announced the guidelines and ground rules which are experienced as promoting expression and interaction.

The leader has also — in this initial phase — encouraged group members to focus on the theme-elicited phenomena which are related to inner and interactional responses. Interpersonal energy flows in an alternating current of awareness and consciousness.

Episodes and Comments: Middle Phase

Event numbers 9 through 30 cover the main stage of the TCI experience. Illustrated here is the dynamic development of the intrapsychic events, the group interactions, and the theme. The basic tasks of the leader are balancing the production of I, We, and It responses — a pacing function. Members are asked to participate chiefly in the shaping function by providing their own most authentic responses, both cognitive and affective.

9. David-Leader-Elaine. Autonomy interfering with someone else has to be curtailed. "Then again," says Elaine, "if you want to make a special point ideologically, you may invite punishment or sanction, but you've made your mark."

10. Frank-David-Leader-Elaine. While Frank amplifies definition of autonomy, leader stresses the concept that autonomy and interdependence are interwoven and can hardly be viewed separately. Elaine's "lack of self-discipline" is the key to her weakened autonomy.

11. Leader brings in reality as a factor that leads to neglect of interdependence as well as to false autonomy (example: staying up late to work).

12. Leader clarifies Alice's difference between dependence and interdependence while Grace asserts that the more interdependent she is, the more autonomous she is.

13. Leader pointedly declines to answer Alice's question to discourage dependency and encourage self-statement.

14. Frank-Charles. Important cognitive point is raised that *understanding* a relationship leads to *less* dependency. Also the more relationships you have, the less dependent you are on any one of them.

The theme is being examined more deeply and introspectively. Members and leader begin to relate themselves and the theme, while learning more about themselves and the theme at the same time. Instead of "free associations" we have here associations directed by the force of the theme. Although content predominates, this is far from an ordinary discussion. The positive tone set with great care by the leader has promoted an active, seeking quality by more than half of the group members. The leader, by declining to answer a question, has made it possible for the questioner's dependency to be viewed within the context of the theme and interaction.

15. Harry gains insight and grasp of autonomy by clarifying a recurrent feeling: by accommodating himself to his father's tragedy, he was in fact not being *autonomous* but only carried along by his environment. Leader underlines Harry's experience in getting something for himself. Elaine also admires his use of autonomy in the current revelation.

The TCI method does not rule out or deny the past as material for a living-learning experience. Illustrated here is Harry's joining the theme to integrate an unresolved burden of not having understood his accommodation to an early tragedy.

16. Leader feels that Elaine and others are talking too much to her. Others deny this, but immediately following, there is a stepped-up interaction.

Leader, in a balancing move, acts to shift the center of the group away from her and toward others and the theme.

17. Flowing from this act is strong interaction around the rules of breaking in and being "one's own chairman," as though leader had apprised them of their excessive dependence on her and now the group members were taking matters into their own hands.

18. Leader picks up a side remark Frank had been making to Blanche; Frank and Charles have agreed that they have no strong feelings of invasion of privacy or being controlled because their tapes were circulated.

19. After Alice agrees that Frank comes out looking good on tapes, Grace brings up a "disturbance" about not having participated in workshops. Leader tries to relieve the disturbance paradigmatically by asking for something Grace doesn't want on tape, and wishes that the group would help Grace. Alice points out that Grace "doesn't resolve"; David gets her to realize that she fears she would be "annihilated" through an interchange with group.

The TCI group is described as a living-learning experience. If anyone, including the leader, absents himself in anger, withdrawal, or preoccupation, a link in the chain of interaction and coherence is disconnected. Bringing a person back to the group from inner or outer distractions takes precedence. It is at first difficult for the participant to realize that he *is* participating by being distracted and announcing it. The better each participant accepts and works within this rule, the more he can develop his autonomy and authentic participation. By breaking in or by bringing in a disturbance, the person has opened two doors to rejoining the group. First, expressing the disturbance may dispel it. Second, the distraction might consist of feelings which in fact do have a not easily recognized connection with the theme.

20. Grace admits openly to her need for interdependence, and for a while Alice and Frank do not recognize this but see her as they did in the past. Leader intervenes to clarify Grace's *current* behavior in group: "Grace is saying she'd like to feel different and needs help for this."

21. Elaine and Ike intensify their current perceptions of Grace, that she comes across as dissociated: evil and good all mixed. This perception helps Grace feel her own sadness (over this existential blurring), and leader asks her first for what she wants and then to go around and *be understood* the way she wants to be understood.

22. As Grace goes around, leader picks up in her delivery a *cause* for her dissociation, namely that she treats herself as a "case-history"; this revelation brings closure and peace.

23. SILENCE

In psychotherapy, pathology is the main "theme"; in a TCI group, growth and learning are the chief underlying themes. The leader here invited Grace to "get on top" of her pathology — the dissociated feelings — by asking her to deal with her healthy potential. She was encouraged to ask fellow group members to understand her the way she wants to be understood. The ensuing silence may be seen as a respectful and productive pause for assimilating the new perceptions of Grace.

24. After Harry felt relieved by the peace, John describes the episode above with Grace as most meaningful. In part he shared the experience of the group reaching out to Grace. He couldn't go any further despite Harry's and Ike's efforts but was involved deeply by crying.

25. Leader intervenes to stay with John: her intuition and fantasy say that John would tend *not* to take home his experience from workshop. But John denies this feeling. He keeps alluding vaguely to how he *has* used the feelings in the group for his benefit and "feels better for it." Others are still puzzled about what he got out of it. Finally leader turns to Charles and his silence, but this act was disregarded.

26. The air seems to be cleared by the group's pursuit of John. This clearing was expressed by Grace whose body movement was noted by leader. Blanche wondered about the effect of Grace's revelation on group — at one time in the past this sort of thing was a relief for her. John then explained that Grace's revelation helped him participate inwardly.

If there were a "TCI scale of behavior," this group would score high in these events. The "working through" of the theme has resulted in a living out of some of its benefits (autonomy and interdependence). John strives to the utmost to reach out to another member, with others helping him. The group respects John's own style of experiencing benefit by not forcing him into the majority mold of verbalization. Several group members join cooperatively to produce a new constellation of individuals interacting freely and adventurously.

27. Leader's intervention aims at getting the focus off the individual. To this end, leader asks if everyone *autonomously* wanted to focus on Blanche.

Where there occurs an undue emphasis upon one of the elements of the I-We-It triangle, the leader, as a balancer, may notice this state more quickly than other group members and has the task of interrupting or intervening. Here the attention on Blanche took on an interviewing or "therapizing" form which went off the track of the theme. The leader brought the theme into focus by suggesting that the *autonomy* of the group members was not really being exercised at this point.

28. Group brings itself back to the point where leader called attention to Charles' silence. Obvious to several members was Ike's attempt at blocking attention to Charles.

29. Leader reports she had David in mind a few times because of his silence. David's answer that he was concerned about having to leave sooner was lost in view of the following interchange with Charles.

30. Ike turns to Charles who admits he is afraid of being left out. Leader interprets this exchange in light of a previous report about his parents' excluding him from the dining room unless he behaved well. Leader: "If you behave like a 'good boy,' you get adult attention; if you behave like a 'troublemaker' but authentically, you won't get attention." Charles agrees, but qualifies.

Group members continued to explore themselves authentically in the context of the theme. Charles' confusion about self-assertiveness was suggested by the leader, who recalled one of Charles' earlier accounts. He has had a lifelong dilemma: "good," acceptable behavior is forced and inauthentic; disruptive behavior is more true and autonomous. In this group he had held back so as not to feel "disruptive." Charles seemed to get the full impact of this enacted insight.

Episodes and Comments: Ending Phase

31. Elaine expresses such fondness for leader as to be embarrassed.

32. Group members become aware of their characteristic mode of getting what they want from each other.

33. Leader confronts two of the participants with their persistent dependency on her, to help organize their feelings.

34. Agreed-upon time to stop arrives. Members exchange warm "goodbyes" before leaving the room for their destinations.

The ending phase should, if possible, leave each member with the feeling that he has been self-actualizing and has led a balanced life within the group. Optimally, in this phase intrapsychic and interpersonal distractions to communication, learning, and integration have been aired and minimized. Attempts have been made to resolve group interaction. In this workshop the pursuit of autonomy and interdependence has resulted in the participants' increased awareness of and growth in giving and receiving, separating and joining. The TCI leader has also aimed at encouraging the development of the members, even after the group experience, by dealing with some of the problems of separation.

Detailed Flow of the Galveston Group

This is only the beginning and relatively brief segment of the Galveston Group workshop on "Autonomy and Interdependence." There will be observed flashes and hints of processes usually revealed in a more advanced stage of a functioning TCI group. This fact may be explained by the group behavior of psychologically sophisticated members. Yet frequent observations of and experiences with different cultural and age groups — often including "non-veteran" group participants — demonstrate that the very same process can develop, if at a slower pace.

In this analysis we offer a microscopic view of the moving current of events in the Galveston Group. Here we attempt to provide the more precise flavor of what is said by the participants and leader, as well as the perceptions, deductions, and intuitions of the leader with respect to content and process.

THE GALVESTON GROUP
"Autonomy and Interdependence"

Protocol	Outline of Process	Comments on Content and Process [1]
1. Leader: Theme is Autonomy and Interdependence. (After defining these terms briefly, leader asks for silent thinking about theme as pertaining to personal and professional practice.) What does it mean for each of us and for our patients. Autonomy means my choice of what I want to do. Interdependence is my relationship with others, their dependence on me, and vice-versa. (Two minutes of silence)	State the theme.	The theme is stated by the leader at the outset of this theme-centered interactional workshop. In this instance, she chooses to offer her own definitions — in the simplest and most eliciting manner.
2. Leader: Now for a second silence. Close your eyes and concentrate on body sensations. (Lists all parts of the body.) Try to stay with the sensations of	Every silence has a specific function. Eyes closed: inner awareness.	Be aware of your body; let body-sensations serve as accompaniment for the feelings. "I loaf and I invite my soul." (Whitman)

Protocol	Outline of Process	Comments on Content and Process
your body and relaxation of your body and feel the wholeness of your body. Let your mind wander by itself and let your feelings wander . . . whatever you want to think about or feel about, do. . . . (Two minutes of silence)		The leader is shaping this directed silence to the specific theme. Thus the silence serves as a particular invitation to this theme.
3. Leader: Now for a third silence. Keep your eyes closed. When you open them soon, each one of you meet each person's eyes in this room for a few seconds or as long as necessary, just enough to make contact. Remain silent. Open your eyes. The rule of all interactional workshops is to give to the group and to oneself and to get from the group as much as one can and to be responsible for doing that . . . to be the chairman of yourself.	Leader helps participants toward interaction. "Give and get."	Speaks of making "contact" with other after having found one's "center." The light touch. Stating the ideals in the course of the workshop; they are the other side of the coin of its ground rules.

Protocol	Outline of Process	Comments on Content and Process
(Two minutes of silence)		
4. (Alice: Describes a nice warm feeling but also difficulty in glancing at others . . .)	Tone of group responds to theme —letting it happen.	She feels awareness of her inner physical state; is loathe to interact.
5. John: Interdependence scares me more than autonomy . . . I have more trouble with that.	Thematic response: Leader lets group ease into its work.	The impact of feeling himself into the suggested mode of experiencing "scares me," he shares.
6. (David tells joke about animals doing "their thing.")		In this case, paying attention to bodily sensing at the start is heuristic for participant's freedom to share a joke with libidinal overtones.
7. (Harry tells story about porcupines who got together for warmth, but whose quills made them separate.)	Theme is reflected.	Porcupines can be "dependent" on a horizontal plane, in keeping with their animalness; autonomy in our sense is out of the question, except for human beings.
8. Frank: Autonomy conflicts with interdependence. In an agency, if I'm more authentic, I	The particular emerges to make real the general.	The way I see the theme: Being more authentic carries with it some threat to smooth teamwork. Explora-

Protocol	Outline of Process	Comments on Content and Process
run into danger of not being enough interdependent. When you work for an agency and your values don't correspond with agency and I am authentic, I'm liable to be fired or restricted. . . . Therefore there is less autonomy and less choice of where to work. On the other hand, if I am less authentic and more conforming, I have more freedom of choice because I fit into the system.		tory mode. Can I be my true self and not censured by a group of pedestrian conformity?
9. David: I think mine is sort of different. I see achieving autonomy as coming out of interdependence. I see interdependence coming before autonomy. Maybe you are thinking of this place. I didn't feel interdependence, acceptance in this place; I didn't feel accepted as a person, and I isolated myself.	The cognitive "It" is in focus.	Another viewpoint.

Protocol	Outline of Process	Comments on Content and Process
10. Harry: I get out there too far, and then fear being cut off.	The cognitive is effectively meshed with an "I" statement.	Candidness may make for loneliness.
11. Charles: Authentic people sometimes get autonomy restricted; criminals may be included in this.		Now "autonomy" is pursued as theme.
12. John: In order to exercise autonomy, I have to know what it is I want. Sometimes I find I'm afraid to know this.	Speaks for "I."	An "I" begins to emerge, but as is "par for the course," not quite here/now at first blush.
13. Elaine: I experience this thing somehow in the way of pressure to feel what I don't feel. I can do what I don't feel. I can do what the other person wants, even cheerfully, but I can't feel it or want it. And there are certain spontaneous things people want me to feel and then I can't cooperate. I	The "We" corner of the I-We-It triangle.	The leader is accepting: here we are given a "catalogue of behaviors" set forth but not felt here/now. Now the member speaks about being a member in *this* group; I want you to get to know me.

Protocol	Outline of Process	Comments on Content and Process
can get coffee cheerfully, but I couldn't act lovey-dovey with some of the people here who want me to.		
14. Grace: I fear that if I express my case, it won't be received appropriately, and that interferes with relating and being dependent. I feel some admiration for you, as a leader, that when we started mediating, you could do that.	From explicit here/now input to I/you dialogue.	Moving to openness on a somewhat deeper level. Leader is effective here in using restraint on a wish to make *it* happen too fast or *my* way. The dividend is that the individuals move on pathways of their own choice or making.
15. David: I was anxious when the two of you were fighting before the session began.	Triad to new dyad.	Observing interesting moment of two people getting together . . . makes for own interaction with the "prime-movers."
16. Grace: I still feel anxious. My experience was sort of rejection or something . . . anxiety.	Feelings take the spotlight from cognition.	Here/now "feel anxious" statement, timidly rejecting feeling of rejection. . . . If I come on too strong about being rejected, I may stand out inappropriately even now.

Protocol	Outline of Process	Comments on Content and Process
17. David: I don't like it a damn bit that tapes of Fred Diamond's workshop were circulated.	Disturbances take precedence.	Bold, simple statement of where I stand. Stimulates airing of buried distraction of others.
18. Grace: I objected to the tape recorder because after the first workshop with Fred, tapes were circulated.	Pairing.	Grace feels as David does: Behind my back other(s) tampered with my autonomy. Real grievance.
19. David: It was? Elaine, you ought to object.		A trio is emerging: new energy center in the group's gestalt.
20. Leader: This is erasing the last tape of Fred.	Deals with disturbance enough to bring members back to theme.	Attempt to agree about a previous violation of the group's autonomy.
21. Harry: This is what is scary about interdependence. It leads to exploitation.		Interdependence is a task, not just an academic preoccupation.
22. Ike: I don't think you really understand - - - Alice (interrupting): I'm just re-		

Protocol	Outline of Process	Comments on Content and Process
sponding to you, Harry. You are so real. I just want to touch you.		
23. Grace: Fred Diamond's workshop doesn't matter. It is what has to be done *now* that matters, which has alienated me. I don't like me when I'm like this.	Dyadic gestalt* of theme flow.	She has reached out at a higher level from her earlier solipsistic gestalt* of theme flow.
24. Leader: I was disappointed yesterday when you didn't want to make the decision, and now you don't seem to be back where you were yesterday.	Leader minimizes transference by stating own feelings.	Leader assumes group is ready to proceed beyond the disturbance.
25. Alice: I didn't want to fight with you, Grace. . . . I don't like you. I resented what happened because it was my tape-recorder, and you coupled me with somebody who circulated the tapes.	Theme emerges as group experience.	Fighting is an interaction only when I accept our interdependence. "I am too proud to fight" suggests a deficiency in interdependence.
26. Charles: This is the sort of situa-		Supports anger, but self-energy

tion I would get very angry about if I were you, Alice.

flags before he can get to thrust with his own feeling.

27. Alice: Part of this is my difficulty, two extremes. I want to get something for myself, and secondly I didn't want to argue with Grace . . .

Can't make encounter.

Easier to talk about relationship than risk it to deepen it.

28. Leader: I'm still struck with your pessimism. . . . It's like you're saying, 'whenever I'm dependent on someone else's changing his mind, he will not, she will not.'

Timing.

Leader chooses this as the moment to "reflect" and clarify.

29. Alice: I can go further than that. Whenever I'm dependent on anyone, it never works out. Interdependence is *my* problem. I seldom count on anyone for anything.

"This is the way I am."

30. Leader: You count on the *negative*, that nothing will work.

Confronts, but with light touch.

Leader's effort to sharpen focus of self-awareness and invite change during this workshop.

Protocol	Outline of Process	Comments on Content and Process
31. Ike: Self-fulfilling prophecy. I now see a resolution. You asked Grace a question		
32. Grace: We tried that. I don't like Alice; we don't try each other. I'm sorry I don't trust.		Softening of impasse awareness, so to speak: "I suffer being me."
33. Alice (to Grace): I would trust you if you had a tape-recorder. . . . I don't like what I've seen of you in workshops, and that's all I've seen. The cop-out, the tease, come in late, pull back, can't be trusted to get involved with. That's something very important with me.	Making the theme reality by practicing autonomy.	From a recognizing-confrontation to an exploring-encounter.
34. (Male members talk about trusting Grace and Alice.)		
35. Alice: I should think that what Grace and I are talking about is different from what others are refer-	Formation of new "being me with you."	This is fostered by "we are closer now that we are fighting than you (rest of the group) are, just being

Protocol	Outline of Process	Comments on Content and Process
ring to.		onlookers." Relating at a syntaxic* level.
36. Leader: I understand one thing which I had in mind. Emotionally, I understand what Alice said, 'I don't like you, but I would trust you with the tape-recorder.' I was thinking, Grace . . . I was hoping you'd fight it out. I was thinking, I don't see how you would distrust Alice's statement that she wouldn't play it.	Not merely reactive* or active,* but interactive.*	Leader is open about her own wishes and thought processes, eschews use of gimmicks.
37. Grace (to Alice): I have to take back something else. I don't dislike you. . . . I'm sorry you don't like me.	The dyadic process has become the predominant trend of centering. Leader will now shift away from this.	Candor tends to be contagious.
38. Leader: I feel we're back to yesterday's topic: all Jews are bad, all tape-recorders are going to go out . . . an erasing of individuality.	From the then to now. From the dyadic trend to the free association of individuals.*	Leader lends a more precise cognitive process.

Protocol	Outline of Process	Comments on Content and Process
39. Blanche: You make me very uncomfortable too, L.; I alternately go toward you and move away from you. I go toward you when I sense your discomfort but I turn away from you, Grace, when you make others uncomfortable.	Insightful statement in light and warmth of the theme.	
40. Leader: What does the heartbeat say?	Holistic philosophy of TCI.	Leader uses gestalt approach (Perlsian) epitomizing at this moment the appeal to body sensing and language to give substance to our "conversation" in group interaction.
41. Blanche (thoughtful silence): Probably a little bit of uncertainty about speaking . . . words won't come out right . . . words tumble out backwards . . . Is it worth saying?		Response to "What does the heartbeat say?"
42. Leader: 'What will they think about me?'		Leader paraphrases to support her risk of becoming more clearly aware of herself (above).

Protocol	Outline of Process	Comments on Content and Process
43. Blanche: Oh, it's that I was wondering about autonomy for me, and for you, Harry. You are very autonomous, and I have a lot of interdependence and I'm striving for autonomy. My autonomy is craziness, a different kind than yours.	I-We-It in becoming.	Useful component of a TCI group. "Appreciating and valuing differences" is often a benchmark of a good workshop. Self awareness and consciousness of others are developed.
44. Harry: You don't look like you are crazy.		
45. Elaine: People say I'm crazy, talking to people in Holland more than my family — How crazy do you get! I'm missing something. (She gives a sample of so-called "crazy behavior.") It's a momentary thing . . . revelling in associations. Although I got angry looks from Grace, I feel more confidence now, just being myself in this group. It's not so frightening now that I've begun to know some of you better.	Approaching plus level:* shared atmosphere of acceptance leading to willingness to reveal self in new ways.	Dares to be more "open" than ordinary social interaction will allow for or support. Flowering of the "I."

Summary of the Galveston Group in Action

Glancing back to the Galveston Group — protocol and comments — we can review the highlights of a TCI group in action. Individuals with a common interest or task formed voluntarily in response to an announcement. Their chief common interest was learning more about the group work experience and the TCI method. The theme "Autonomy and Interdependence" was selected by the leader for this reason. Another way of expressing the theme could have been "Being Myself and a Group Member in a TCI Group." This was the background and setting which includes the "globe" or the space within which the I-We-It triangle functions.

We saw the humanistic philosophy of the TCI method revealed by the respect given to feeling and immediacy in the learning situation. We illustrated the holistic aspect of this learning through the dynamic development of the person and his interactions with the theme in focus at all times. Departures from the theme were treated as necessary and even desirable where the disturbing feelings had a subtle connection to the theme or where those distractions not connected to the theme were necessary to free the participant for the job that had to be done.

The leader's role in balancing and shifting the personal, interactional, and thematic elements was amply represented. The guidelines and ground rules for all were frequently underlined.

Finally, the current of the group life was described in phases — first, middle, and ending — to help the reader understand the timing of certain group events and the leader's interventions.

VIII

Five
Pathways
to
Achievement

Why Five Modes?

Groups are described in terms of specific purpose or process: a task group, a "buzz session," a planning committee, a "think-tank." We have articulated another useful formulation which goes according to varieties or *modes*. These modes represent particular at-this-time and in-this-place needs of individuals in groups. They correspond to an overall emphasis or goal agreed upon by members and leader. While all these modes may appear in any one workshop, the leader usually stays with one particular emphasis in the light of the group's needs and goals.

The five varieties of workshop may be identified as these:

1. exploratory (discovering),
2. expediting (doing),
3. experiential (making connections between inner and outer),
4. experimental (choosing alternatives),
5. evaluational (assessing and deciding on further improvement).

If these approaches to living, working, and relating are already well known and widely employed, we now offer to gear them with the TCI method. By virtue of its flexibility and special ground rules, the TCI method can utilize these modes in their fullest sense by adapting theme and interaction to the specific purpose. Thus a "buzz group" which is designed for exploration may not ordinarily have place for some experiential responses, while a TCI exploratory group has a built-in readiness for this effective concomitant. Or a group process experience may not provide the necessary, built-in cognitive element (to articulate what is being learned), whereas a TCI experiential group can easily invite this cognitive thrust while maintaining the experiential mode. In effect the TCI ingredients add more dimension to any group thrust. The Galveston Group, in Chapter VII, had first an exploratory and then an experiential tone.

In offering these modes, we also provide a construct which cuts across existing groups (therapy, guidance, education) and demonstrates the common grounds which we have always sensed but not quite articulated. The psychotherapist and the teacher do indeed have a lot in common when each, in his way, explores emotional strengths or intellectual assets. One of the actual differences lies in the varied combinations and emphases of our modes. In this light we speak of the therapist who can pursue the experiential and experimental to their reasonable limits, while the teacher may engage the student more in a search for exploratory and expediting limits.

A methodological bonus in the use of modes is the conscious footing it provides for the particular purpose of the group. More often than not a group is blown off course by ambiguity of purpose or by individual needs which have been harnessed to an agreed-upon overall purpose but not to a specific way of getting there.

1. Exploratory

This style, structured for a maximum of discovery, is related to Dewey's learning by exploring and doing. Each participant is invited to find the particular relevance to himself of the announced theme — which has a general relevance for the participants. The emphasis here is to uncover relationships in language or process, to enter new cognitive and conative territory.

In exploring his career, a student may construct this living map by considering how he wants to become and be a lawyer. The TCI approach leaves room for the parallel exploration of getting to know one another. "To whom am I most drawn?" "Do I feel a twinge of distrust toward someone present?" This mode is appropriate to beginning, orientational situations to lay the groundwork for any desired personal or social enrichment. The first session of any new group, for any purpose, can succeed more when an explicit exploratory mode is agreed upon and guided by a leader.

The theme for the exploratory mode — as usual — is stated within a warm and easygoing ambiance. The leader in his manner and intent thereby animates the free improvisation of dyads. Once the group members have made a theme meaningful for each other through risks of seeing life differently and encounters of feeling similar, we have the basic ingredients of an exploratory workshop. The reader will find in the beginning account of the "Galveston Group" (Chapter VII) a model of exploratory statements about the theme. We have often conducted workshops with the theme "Getting to Know You, Letting You Know Me." Here we have strengthened the freedom to explore truly without having to prove oneself. Tensions typically engendered by group experience are related, giving way to a freer, more recreational feeling and posture about just being together and being oneself.

Whom do we see achieving high dividends from participation in an exploratory phase of a workshop or in an exploratory series of workshops? Consider the person fearful of a frontal invasion of his defensive walls; or the person who inhibits himself because of the prospect of discomfort and embarrassment; or the person who, not taking the time or leisure, has closed out much of the perceptual field. He can literally have his eyes opened to a terrain he did not previously dare to explore fully. The child, adolescent, or adult passing through succeeding developmental phases may find it necessary to see and understand himself in the context of such a framework. Through an exploratory workshop he could best gain a first-hand view and experience of where he is in relation to these personal-cultural criteria.

This free relating of elements of knowledge and experience has its special relevance and importance to classroom teaching and learning. Where the classroom themes are almost exclusively content oriented, the exploratory workshop enables the student to become a more active learner. This mode gives freer rein to spontaneous activity as a counterweight to the typical passive learning that takes place. The exploratory mode with its emphasis upon discovery has special value for the beginning counselee who needs the freedom to reconnoiter his problems while reinforcing his desire for help.

2. Expediting

The plagues of our time for children and youth — apathy, indifference to finding work as a pleasurable task, difficulty in clarifying life goals, forced lengthening of the school years, in some cases to the late twenties — are all of great concern to legislators, scientists, and educators. The purpose of the expediting workshop is to clarify these dilemmas, ambivalences, and impasses whenever possible. Emphasis is placed on "What can we do well?" leading to "What will I do"; "What am I ready to do?" This mode of interaction introduces a time schedule and the rigors of an agenda. Now after an exploratory phase, there is readiness to work. The proviso as usual is that the individual's disturbance or distraction takes precedence; no one presumes to know the others' minds. Emphasis in this "staging process" is on the present becoming the future. Sensations and perceptions are used to feed the expediting mode. Finding a richer experience in the work of the expediting workshop the participant can hopefully develop a hunger for more work experiences which are equally intense and rewarding.

The model of the kibbutz reminds us of the motivational force attained by the group task. The necessity of getting the job done is recognized as synonymous with individual freedom. In the expediting workshop the member witnesses how the job has taken over the habitual energies of all the participants. For example we have the notes of a fifth grade social studies class. The teacher with a living-learning approach met first with a committee of pupils to establish a relevant theme. They decided on "Knowing and Being Part of My

Community." Following this gathering, the class met in theme-centered interactional sessions around this theme. In the first few sessions the exploratory mode was emphasized: "What is the importance of the task?" "What is the meaning of this task now for our development?" Following this stage, the TCI teacher employed the expediting phase until completion of the project five weeks later. The pupils interacted and participated in the following tasks:

1. interest sub-groups were formed;
2. selected and accepted background material was read;
3. specific field trips were planned and undertaken;
4. children brought back reports to the others;
5. each student digested his own experience and shared it with the others.

To provide additional feel for the workings of an expediting workshop with specific individuals, we offer the following examples:

a) In a counseling group the TCI counselor was presenting certain favored modes for her clients. An immature, anxious, hysterical graduate student with serious problems in meeting work deadlines was asked to concentrate on the expediting mode. His tendency to be excessively labile was counterbalanced by learning and adopting the role of a committed participant who takes responsibility for the pace and direction of the session.

b) In a junior. high school classroom, a teacher noticed that Cathy and Ceri were high achievers but lone workers, never giving or taking in group learning. A TCI guidance worker invited them to an expediting workshop on "My Ideas about the Coming Prom." Here the members of the group were invited to augment their intellectual skills with the necessary social-emotional ingredients. Cathy and Ceri were called upon to enlist in what they could do with others. They felt deeply how their clever and original ideas were accepted in this workshop as they became associated with the thoughts and personalities of the others.

c) We know of many people of all ages who have squandered much of their talent because they "could not complete the task." Their dependency, or other pertinent dynamics related to identification, existential anxiety, or inability to narrow perceptual vectors, prevented them from assuming the successful, more important role of the "doer." Many such people, in our experience, were encouraged finally to get to work purposefully through the channel of identifying and building the interdependence they were nearly capable of but which had been undeveloped. In these cases the expediting workshop succeeded through the powerful instrumentality of encouraging total involvement in an expediting theme, requiring a working-doing-achieving orientation.

3. Experiential

This mode is best timed after one has achieved a place in a school, community, family, or work group. Now comes the chance to take pleasure in and acknowledge the fruits of exploring and expediting. The emphasis is not so much a cognitive ramification of the theme as it is a living out of the I and We. The *now* pervades the theme. This is where we want to "sink the gusher." Best effects have resulted where individuals are seeking better ways of relating, communicating and growing together. Valiant efforts — only partly successful — have been made by members of the same organization to have "sensitivity group experiences" together, only to find the "big real world" of organizational politics and power priorities stamping out the results of their experiential group experience. Ideally, an experiential workshop for healthy families and other groups of mutually accepting and closely knit peers can raise levels of consciousness and personal well-being.

The hallmark of the TCI experiential mode — as of all other modes — is its esthetic and life-connected quality. We stay clear of isolated games, exercises, minilabs (all rightly designed to encourage direct encounter and dialogue), unless the activity has a TCI connection with a theme. With this theme, we nail down the encounter, the confrontation, the nonverbal insight, the physical sensation to the mainstream of thought, emotion, and interaction.

Obviously the person who most needs the experiential style of workshop or experiential style of functioning in any group is one who brings very little of himself to a situation. We are familiar with these dull, depressed, uninvolved, detached, constricted persons in various roles, situations, and efforts. They need help to "open up" — not be cracked open — to the possibilities that they may act, react, and interact with much more than the weak solo notes they have been sounding.

The process encouraged in the experiential workshop is to increase one's posture of readiness to take in any and all sense data from one's human and natural surroundings. These data are then matched with the vibration which the participant finds resonating within himself in a leisurely, receptive atmosphere. The workshop leader is determined to invite the release of more energy in this mode from unexpected sensory and emotional sources. There is no encumbrance of carrying the burden of a narrow focus on work objectives (as required in other modes). Energy release is transmitted back and forth and hopefully implanted as additional assets and sources of pleasure and competency within each person.

4. Experimental

New adaptations to changing situations are perhaps the key to human and, in general, biological survival. This workshop mode aims at survival and, beyond that, increased efficiency in functioning. These workshops present opportunities to play with new ways of overcoming barriers and to cross new thresholds of effectiveness. Here freedom is the recognition of necessity. Unfettered combinatorial (creative) thinking may bring together elements which had seemed utterly disparate up to now. Periodic experimenting to find essential parsimony in work, as well as delighting in far-fetched innovative alternatives, helps us to avoid hardening of categories and to keep open unchartered pathways of spontaneity. Old relationships with friends and colleagues may prove anachronistic in the light of different rates of personal development. With new ways open in friendship and in doing things, we are free to recognize and release new synergies into actual products. Every organization seeks a way out of stagnation when things have become routine. The experimental workshop, encouraging change, may give people the key to the way out of such debilitating humdrum.

Among those who stand to benefit most from an experimental mode are the down-the-middle people rather inflexible, yet effective in their organizations, who are unaware of the real possibilities of innovation. How often on vacation do they briefly taste the passing thrill of doing things differently, but then they return to an encapsulated, programmed life about which they bitterly complain. Then too there are dreamers — of every age — and those who feel exaggeratedly different. They need a chance to translate their fantasies and fears into new workable plans for more active involvement with others. The idiosyncrasies of others, when shared in an experimental workshop, may be openly admired and used productively for the introduction of constructive novelty in work and play.

If a given workshop experience is specifically geared to experimentation and change using the power of a TCI approach, chances are greater that people and organizations can change. In a college class a knowledgeable TCI instructor was unable to change the passive and "watching-for-grades" attitudes of students without instituting a long-term and intensive workshop on "Changing Myself for the Better as a Student." It was here that certain students, having long felt that their own learning methods were efficient, discovered that they were unsuitable and unadaptive to the learning situation of the rest of the class with whom they were supposedly engaged in a joint project. These students discovered the anachronism and replaced it in the context of actual accomplishment *with* classmates. Others in the group who were manifestly more committed to the work of the class admitted to their lost joy in work. Discovering that they were not being sufficiently related to the "I" of their work (that is, veering off in certain more favored directions of their own), they experimented with "doing their own thing." They were surprised to find even more acceptance, respect, and involvement with the others.

5. Evaluational

The burden of this workshop is to view — in a calm way — the streams of life activity (working, loving, and thinking) that I/We have been accomplishing. From our vantage point on higher land, we survey our avowed purposes and allow for the possibility that a new design is called for to continue the pattern of a purposeful life.

In the course of the evaluational workshop, we enjoy the tangible concomitants of our work and are free to criticize ourselves, the task, and each other, with full mutual acceptance. Each member may grasp this opportunity to look back to the history of what he is evaluating and to plan the stages toward re-creation.

Presumably every organization engages in some form of self-evaluation, whether it be only the head of the organization who confers with a few others in charge or whether there be a greater effort to involve more people in planning conferences. Considering the massive resistance to change, a universal phenomenon, the purpose and process of an evaluational experience are subject to weighty opposition, whether on the part of individuals or organizations. The question, "How are you; how is it going?" can be answered in the affirmative or negative when a one-word answer is called for. But to answer this for someone who cared really to hear your answer, you need time, trust, and insight into how it really "is going." The special advantage of this TCI mode is that we can involve more individual assessments in a given group than is usually the case in a meeting of this kind, because of the drawing power of the stated central theme.

We provide a list suggesting those individuals who would benefit from participating in a TCI evaluational workshop chiefly because the important function of the "examined life" has been missing from their lives.

a) Those who are not future oriented, who do not plan ahead, who cling unrealistically and anxiously to the feeling that "everything will work out," who fear that what they are doing cannot stand study and change.

b) Those who need to exercise their cognitive processes at more advanced levels, in terms of "How can I accomplish what I am doing in light of broader goals and better results?"

c) Children for whom the workshop could provide one of the first experiences in guided self-awareness; a chance to practice an objective viewing of themselves — to begin to see themselves as a process, growing toward something and away from something; a chance to review their developmental tasks in terms of what they are ready for next. Thus a workshop on "Doing Homework for Myself" for twelve-year olds could relate to the beginnings of adolescent separation from parent.

Modes in Their Natural Order

Now consider the possibility that these five modes constitute a natural sequence, both in the process of everyday living-learning in the social matrix and in the general process of a session's or group's development. The steps individuals take to become viable groups under skilled leadership often parallel the normative stages of becoming autonomous people.

In approaching a new situation, the student, worker, teacher, manager and counselor go through an *exploratory* experience. In the TCI context this orientational experience becomes more alive, since it goes hand in hand with getting to know and letting oneself be known by others in similar plight and mood. Anxiety is lessened, and the road is smoothed for *expediting* more intractible tasks.

This *expediting* mode serves individual and group needs to clarify tasks. Ambivalent feelings about doing them are worked out, and psychological space and time are given to rehearse complex activities in thoughts and feelings in a safe group environment. Now the member can feel more accepted as he really functions, not as he sees fit to function. Genuine criticism is accepted; reciprocal honesty is more practical. The previous sense of narcissistic injury gives way to a feeling of a constructive clash of work and interactional styles in an effort to make viable the most felicitous synergism.

The group member can now dare to — and is more ready to — function in the *experiential* mode. He is free to get in touch with new sensory, perceptual, and cognitive connections. This openness readies the participant to become more involved in ongoing and future tasks.

The *experimental workshop* takes on more usefulness after the three preceding phases have been undertaken and when participants have gained skill as effective living-learning members. Now we are ready to assay creative alternatives in styles of work and play. This experimentation includes risking closer personal relationships and their rewards, as well as daring to undertake tasks which seem possible for the first time. When, for example, the "committee" work in a classroom reaches an impasse, this workshop would provide a way to invoke the principle of status-denial in the service of greater self-actualization of the "group ego."

The first four workshop modes reflect the processes by which a person makes the environment his own. Now we assume in the *evaluational* mode that the person is ready and able to accept constructive criticism of himself and his work. To *evaluate* requires the sagacity of one who has emerged from the other modes in the spirit of "resting on the seventh day" seeking replenishment and the energy to go forward.

Each mode has to be seen with regard to the ideals and purposes of the group as well as the overall strategy of conducting it in theme-centered interactional ways. Each mode makes its own contribution to a richer and more articulated experience. In sequence, the exploratory and evaluational clearly mark the initial and completing phases of the TCI concept of group life. The expediting and experiential alternate in a rhythm which closely follows the interrelated needs of accomplishing tasks and being ourselves (experientially) with each other. Which of these two will form the thicker layer of the sandwich depends on the taste and temper of leadership and participation as well as the way the theme is evolving. The experimental workshop requires the added finesse of a scientific attitude of observing, measuring, and — if possible — reproducing phenomena and drawing correct conclusions. The evaluational mode asks not only "What happened?" and "Where are we going?" but also "Why did it happen?" making it the most philosophical of the five.

We believe that modes are more readily employed in the TCI approach than in any other for making the most out of interpersonal and intrapsychic events. Modes can be more easily related to a viable life style, permitting the person to acquire goals and skills according to individual needs and preferences.

IX

Finding
and
Using
Themes

We have not discovered themes; they are in fact all around us. In writing this chapter, our own theme has been related to communicating new ideas to hopefully receptive and involved participants — including readers, editors, and colleagues — while at once maintaining our own style and integrity.

Guidance counselors, teachers, and administrators have always been aware of important tasks and goals, such as orientation, personal development, educational and vocational planning. From the vantage point of the junior high school pupil, these tasks and goals translated into themes may be "What I Would Like to Change about this School if I Could" or " Making Sense with Parents." The evolving themes of many college students today are, for example, finding new ways to expand the mind or new ways to be a woman. While the word "theme" has certainly not been newly invented, the TCI method has perhaps found a way to bottle a theme which is then released in a group as food for thought, feeling, and behavior.

Definition

A *theme* is the subject of focus in a theme-centered interactional (TCI) group where the theme, self, and group are in continuous interplay. Pre-announced or produced by group decision, the theme is stated as immediate, positive, striving, and open-ended to awaken feelings and interest. The object is to stimulate productive cohesion and to provide the initial and ongoing impetus for the cognitive and affective, the interplay of which leads to each person's self-actualizing behavior.

The theme is announced by the prospective leader in response to a problem, a current issue, or a strong, timely interest. Individuals or groups are invited to enroll as they would for any meeting. Or members of a group (club, class, employees, clients) may discover a theme evolving from their experiences and wish to pursue it in a TCI setting. For example, during a meeting with their faculty coordinator, traffic monitors in a sixth grade class became aware of their responsibilities to the school, while having at the same time to deal with their friends and to build their own self-concepts. This confluence of responsibilities could serve as a basis for a theme.

A theme is not a *topic*. One can discuss the question of "drug abuse" cogently, and even with strong feelings, without revealing or sharing any personal relationship to the question.

A theme is not an area of *subject matter,* such as the "U.S. Trust Territory," since the latter points to what can be accomplished alone and merely demonstrated or exhibited in a group.

A theme is not an *agenda.* At a committee meeting, the onus of accomplishing an end is borne, even if the involvement of members dwindles or is absent.

A theme is not a *point of view,* like "Dating for Everyone." Its purpose, rather, is to explore each participant's relevant experiences and awaken differences in point of view.

A theme is not a *panacea* of a proclamation such as "Joy" or "Growth." Such proclamations tend to open wide the gates but the surge of energy may fail to provide practical, lasting change.

Purposes of a Theme

The theme declares the group's focus in a clear, simple, inviting way. Like the title of a book or play, it has to attract its clientele, or at least not discourage them initially. Once the group members have arrived and are chatting expectantly or are nervously silent (in the informal circular seating provided), we can safely assume that a second purpose has been achieved. We now have a group bonded by a common and unifying commitment.

If a third purpose has been met, these very participants have been attracted to the positive and relatively nonthreatening aspects of the theme. Very few people would register for a workshop on the topic of "Perils and Tribulations of Parenthood." However, considerable anxiety and resistance to self-scrutiny would be overcome by the more inviting theme, "Growing as Parents, Children, and People." The example just mentioned suggests another purpose, that of relating people at different levels of age, education, cultural background, and personality. The theme is open to a variety of affective, nonverbal, as well as intellectual styles of response, accommodating a surprisingly variegated group. A final purpose provides the leader with leverage in initiating the group experience. Without having to point to individuals or to deliver monologues or "loosening-up" exercises, the leader invites the participants immediately to relate themselves in various ways to the theme, whether through reflection, association, apperception, or interaction. We have seen groups launched with power and ease as their members and leader began acting and interacting through the medium of the theme.

Advantageous Features and Functions

1. The theme serves as the universal joint within the machinery of a dynamic group which can be inclined toward the personal, interpersonal, and cognitive. Thus, the person can relate in a variety of

ways as he exercises those modes which might be neglected or atrophied.

2. Not only can the individual work harder in a more balanced way, but he marshals more versatility with the theme at center. Group members, with their contrasting responses and interactions, can achieve connections with each other by way of the common focus on the theme. These strong bonds are cemented as the members share the whole range of agonies and ecstasies at appropriate moments.

3. The familiar saying, "Give someone a mask and he will reveal himself more easily," has its parellel if we provide a theme. The person is less conscious of how he is doing but is more spontaneous and productive in what he is doing — in this case, relating to a theme at his own level of facility.

4. Every leader becomes concerned when group members go off the track, expending their energies fruitlessly on diversionary tasks, preoccupations with stubborn problems, or "interviews" with other members, if the leader restates the themes, rather than being viewed as a criticism or a weak reminder, this intervention seems to touch the right chord in bringing the wandering members back to themselves and their appointed task.

5. The TCI group provides one advantage in the study of small-group process which is lacking in many other situations. The use of one theme for one or more groups gives the experimenter the benefit of studying content or process against the constant of the theme.

Finding and Constructing Themes

Finding themes can be as easy as listening to children at lunch, scanning a school newspaper, or observing a faculty-student committee meeting. They may range from personal themes of getting to know each other to all manner of shared tasks of living, to conceptual levels of viewing the world, so long as (in each case) personal participation and needs are not neglected. Constructing a theme requires phrasing at the appropriate level of understanding and setting as well as a formulation (immediate, positive, striving and open-ended) in keeping with the criteria of our definition. Sometimes the paradoxical nature of a theme adds a provocative texture.

To illustrate the flavor of a well-formulated theme, we provide a list classified into the five group modes of exploring, expediting, experiencing, experimenting, and evaluating described in Chapter VIII.

1. *Exploring* (uncovering relationships; making multi-dimensional process maps rather than outline maps). Themes:

Finding My Way in this Group (personal growth)

Discovering What I Can Do Best (skills, career)

Identifying and Removing Emotional Barriers to Learning (academic, informal and social learning)

Diagnosing the Strengths of the College Community (institutional improvement and change)

Being a Teacher, Being a Parent, and Relating to a Child (teacher and parent effectiveness)

2. *Expediting* (emphasizing "What can we do here?" "What can I and am I ready to do now?"). Themes:

Getting Things Done with Others (classroom, job, club, organization)

Making Our Department More Responsive to Student and Faculty Needs (high school and college curriculum)

Understanding Group Procedures as a Classroom Teacher (teaching)

3. *Experiencing* (emphasizing the "now," awareness; enjoying and living out the fact of interaction). Themes:

Being Myself and Relating to Others (coming into a new situation)

Freedom and Responsibility (developing personal values)

Autonomy and Interdependence (functioning in an organization)

Appreciating Differences (community improvement)

4. *Experimenting* (emphasizing testing the limits of alternatives in order to solve persistent problems more effectively or more elegantly). Themes:

Finding New Ways of Teaching Old Subjects (teaching)

Taking Risks in Relating Here and Now (interpersonal)

Discovering New Ways of Discipline with Children (teaching)

5. *Evaluating* (making a living "balance sheet" concerning the work of a given enterprise for a meaningful span of time). Themes:

Evaluating My Role and Experience at Home (parent or child)

Where We've Come — Where We've Been (members of an established group)

Airing and Sharing the School Years (students and school personnel)

My Fraternity and I (members of a club with actual or purported ties)

A workshop announcement is best amplified with a briefly etched statement of the aims and scope of the theme. The accompanying three excerpts will provide a view of actually announced themes at a college. These workshops represent combinations of several of the previously defined modes. The announcements were made to a wide and general audience. As expected with any invitation of this kind, unless followed by personal contacts and explanations, only a few people will come in "cold."

1. To the general student body.
Theme: "Freeing Emotions For Learning"

In this group experience we explore different patterns of learning at college. For a few learning is a joyful act accompanied by growth and change. Others are stuck with their indifference or hostility to written or spoken instruction.

Through the theme-centered interactional method, each participant examines his own patterns of receptivity to new experience and explores the question: "How can I free my emotions for learning?"

2. To education majors.
Theme: "Being Myself and Becoming a Teacher"

Becoming a teacher is a worthwhile and difficult endeavor. Maintaining and expanding one's identity is difficult; it is intimately connected with achieving authenticity as a teacher. To explore relations between these two essential elements in professional development is useful and exciting.

With the above in mind, you are invited to join an experiential workshop in which you will get a chance to express yourself and to experiment with a group situation shared by other teachers-to-be.

3. To student community volunteers.
Theme: "Integrating My Volunteer Work with My Ideas"

While work as a community volunteer is often experienced as mainly giving, you may also be deriving some practical skills and information from your assignment. We wish to extend the value of this educational experience.

Our main purpose in providing an ongoing workshop is to bring together the thoughts and theories learned and researched at the college with your actual volunteer activity in the community. Through this interactional experience we intend to seek ways in which to combine intellectual growth, social feeling, and personal needs through your sharing of experiences with others in the program.

As an outcome of this workshop we anticipate that your personal effectiveness will be enhanced not only as a functioning member of our group; we hope to be of help in the task of channeling your ideas and beliefs into on-the-job action.

What Emerges Through the Theme?

The theme gradually takes on a different form for each person. The emerging sub-theme may be redefined in various ways as the TCI group member pursues his own self-integrating operations. He arrives at his own version of the theme as he relates to it in terms of his own past life and his current interactions.

Just as the theme itself is interpreted according to one's apperceptions, so does it in turn provide growth and change possibilities for the person who is relating to the theme. Serving as a magnetic field, the theme (along with other personal and interpersonal factors) influences the movements of participants and ultimately of the group processes themselves. Group members begin to feel the importance and sustaining quality of the theme. Once this condition has been reached, distractions and diversions may be attended to in a limited way without depleting the main thrust of thematic energy which the group has made its own.

A theme of potentially great value "Gaining Knowledge and Relating to Others" serves as an example of what develops in the use of theme. In a seventh grade class, this theme was offered by the TCI-oriented guidance counselor in response to students' interest in viewing their own specific patterns as learners.

As the discussions developed the TCI workshop leader and members noted various styles of learning. Some students referred to books; others were more involved with life experiences; some straddled the two in a balanced way. Interacting with other types of learners, group members tried out pathways to knowledge which were not habitual but which resulted in novel discoveries about how they learned, retained, and applied knowledge.

The specific behavior of some of the participants was pointedly influenced by the working out of the theme. Joe was observed to be irritable and belligerent when asking for information. He recognized that this attitude was characteristic of how intertwined his learning process and alienation have been in the past. Ruth was intense and alive — an unusual occurrence for her — as she shared in detail her insights in mastering a piano piece. Here Ruth understood that, by virtue of having related warmly to others, she felt released and intellectually stimulated. During one of these workshops, Phil and Steve, the isolates of the group, felt drawn to each other through their common interest as railroad buffs. While they had been vaguely aware of the common interest for six months, they had never been able to express and share the pleasurable involvement of learning *with* others. The theme provided the connections.

X

Through the One-Way Looking Glass

In Chapters VI-IX we have offered TCI principles as well as examples of actual sessions. Let us now take seats in the one-way observation room to view a functioning TCI group. The instructor is conducting an observation by advanced students who have already in recent weeks studied a number of basic interventions by the leader of this workshop together with the responses by participants. The instructor's purpose here is to invite attention to some of the more complex and subtle processes which occur in a theme-centered interactional workshop.

The group members are seen walking through the door to their meeting room. Some are sitting close together; another is talking to the workshop leader rather intensely. A young man is peering at the mirrored wall, both enjoying his own image and having fantasies about the unseen audience.

The instructor reminds the class members that the processes they are about to see are in the main not unique to TCI groups; yet these phenomena are brought out more vividly in the TCI context, just as features on a microscopic slide become visible by the use of stains.

In Chapter VI we introduced TCI process. Here we formulate in greater depth certain group phenomena in theme-centered interactional terms.

Relating at What Levels?

Each individual brings a certain repertory of behaviors into the drama of relating in a group. He carries himself with a gait and characteristic rhythm learned in other situations; he uses known defenses to protect himself from the opening moment to the closing relationship of the group's life.

In Sullivan's terms, some individual members start out by relating to the ebb and flow of their own sensations as the main stream of importance. They seek to stir the senses of others and tend to focus on the flavor of shared perceptions and the play of kinesthetic happenings; their cherished wish is the reciprocal interplay of the foregoing. This style we term *prototaxic* in group functioning.

The *parataxic* style involves the individual with others in ways which mimic or resurrect the family relationships of the formative years. Members who favor this style can waken the I-you forces in group building; at least they bring a free-floating charisma into the interactive mix. At best, we have here the ingredient that makes a group alive with the interpersonal, a cut above the prototaxic. But from a self-actualizing vantage point, the parataxic style may stick at the level of heightened sensibility and not really go anywhere in terms of theme-centered interactive purposes.

The most advanced style of participation is *syntaxic*. When a member connects with his group's process in the light of a minimally distorting eye-to-eye view of reality, he is able to make and to let things happen in a genuine theme-centered interaction. Here energy is freed to pursue precious ideas at one moment and to get to know valued peers at another moment. The awareness is sufficiently alert to sensitize one to "what I am doing with others, how they are responding, and (very nearly) what they want but are not yet ready to say in words." Consciousness of my thoughts and purpose are enjoyable and become cogent to the point of demanding to be lucidly shared. Ideas are now not used for power-plays or tinged with poorly camouflaged competitiveness. At the same time, the need to conform does not make cowards of our unfettered selfhood. This style is most compatible with whole-person interactions.

Flow of Theme

The primary stage of interaction is demonstrated when one person is well aware of what he is sensing (both pleasant and unpleasant feelings.) When the preponderant impact of the theme is that the majority are merely aware of the spontaneous nonverbal flow-of-self but no genuine communication happens, we call it a "solipsistic gestalt" of theme flow. The group suffers from an impoverishment, interpersonally speaking.

There is a crying need for all individuals to reach each other. Isolates first break through hard walls, a la Monte Cristo, and can then take comfort from grasping newly available hands. This manner is the "dyadic gestalt" of theme flow. Let us suppose for a moment that the theme involved "loneliness." Emerson once said that "being alone is beautiful too if only one has someone to talk to about it." The same is true for any kind of "theme"; it is when dyads, an "I-and-you," are formed that the inner life becomes sharable and we really discover the pith and detail of what we feel and think and want.

When each person has allowed himself to experience his own private world of fantasies and sensitivities and dyads of reciprocal sensibility have developed, it remains for the theme to flow freely, building a true "we" as the group shares interconnected phases of sincere encounter. This state we call a "community gestalt." To arrive at this enrichment, there has to be finely attuned leadership, a responsive membership, and a group patience to let individuals move at their natural pace and rhythm.

Trend of Centering

Imbalance of the I-We-It factors is, in principle, always coming about or being put aright. This is the very essence of spontaneous group workings. Consider some typical imbalances which crop up in flowed minutes or hours of a group's life.

Overemphasis on the "I" is typical of people very much group therapized or completely new to group experience. This sense of individual freedom and "doing one's own thing" is a salient feature of revolving participation in any group. There are times when such self-centered behavior constitutes a vitalizing episode. However, if such behavior predominates, it fails to achieve the mobilizing effect which TCI promotes.

Sometimes in a group energy is focused on the transactions between individuals; their major interest is to sharpen the awareness of how people relate to each other. This dyadic or triadic emergence (or enhancement) is the goal for certain group experiences, but "We" alone is not deemed sufficient for TCI.

When interaction lacks verve and people talk out their interpretation of and experiences with the theme, we find the group theme centered in the cognitive sense. Here the dialogue is not fully involving, and the intellectual content is too little energized by the collision and cohesion of whole individuals. It is tempting and safe for some to overdo the "It" in the course of fulfilling their tendency to relate from the neck up and "make friends" without contacting people.

Where the leader lifts responsibility on to his own shoulders, he instantly creates a trend toward a leader-centered group. Busy as a beaver, he asks "leading questions" and does many other things singlehandedly to initiate interaction. Members of his entourage begin looking to his wisdom at every turn. This form of encounter of course falls short of TCI possibilities.

Ideal centering is created by the *free association of individuals.* Here, connections between people are made up of verbal and non-verbal contacts, including thinking, feeling, sensing, and behaving. If these people associations can be conducted with freedom, one neither sacrifices individuality nor needs to foist himself upon others. This ideal of centering is enhanced by the dropping of defences and the adding of creative alternatives toward bringing life to individuals in groups.

Energy-Initiative Thrust

a) There are leaders who push individuals to be or state themselves; often the leader has a clear picture of what he wants to achieve and acts to paint the colors on the pre-sketched canvas he brings to the scene.

b) In certain instances, particular individuals attract the notice of the leader, and he is drawn to their special problems or their flair for group interaction to the exclusion of many less colorful members. Here the main thrust is put into the hands of a few while less initiating members draw back or even hide their full selves as they become the audience for those in the spotlight.

c) Very common in groups where the leader prefers allowing to making things happen, the thrust from member to member emerges randomly as the vital interaction in the group. The leader tends to default his leadership, overrating the importance of group phenomena per se.

d) In some groups, pairing occurs, and the members of the pairs become the main attraction for each other; the initiative of observers to co-relate and form triangles is needed to make newer, more complex interplay.

e) When the changing valence for interaction of the individual moves to serve his interest in himself or another best, there will transpire a shifting from twos to threes, and new dyads will emerge as one flow of encounter is resolved and another flow of dialogue takes center stage.

Minus, Zero, Plus

We can characterize the general levels of a person's or system's functioning approximately as "not well," "all right," and "wonderful." There are swings back and forth to all levels. The "all right" or *zero* condition represents a form of homeostasis during which time group cohesiveness is established while a certain amount of progress is achieved in fulfilling individual and group goals. A group which becomes too comfortable at the cohesiveness experience may end without discovering much of how the "I's" think and feel about the theme and each other.

When distractions or disturbances predominate, the group is functioning *minus* while efforts are made to recognize and resolve the impediment. As the distraction is aired, reduced, or incorporated by the group and as group members struggle for more relevant interactive experience, the level begins to rise toward *zero.*

When participant interaction at the *plus* level is achieved, a group fulfills the ideal of the theme-centered interactional method. This consists of a flowing of events which partake of awareness of self and other in the increasing consciousness of an emerging theme. A bench mark of the *plus* level is an atmosphere of shared acceptance characterized by a willingness to risk untried formulations and closer relationships. In Heath's (1964) term the "reasonable adventurer" has arrived.

React, Act, Interact

The most common kind of behavior in groups is reactive. Individuals respond to an irritating or attractive stimulus in their surroundings, but initiative is seen as the property of some other thing or person. In this structure it is a grateful fact just to stay alive: "I start with my response to an impinging other; ingenuity at surviving I do possess, but I cannot really innovate as a protagonist."

Most of the group life occurs in the mixed range of active members and reactive members with the characteristic frustration and resentment that accompanies passivity and exacerbated forcefulness. As more individuals in a group attain the active status, the members share responsibility for the course the group takes.

In the group which elicits and allows for maximal openness and the willing participation of equals (status denial), we have the pleasurable and productive phenomena of symmetrical interactions. Here we have the fact of consciousness of others balanced with awareness of self. Themes may be pursued and a true dialogue can take place, as new and specially relevant themes and tasks follow.

3

Teaching and Therapeutic Applications

XI

Humanizing Education

A "humanistic" teacher or learner in a current view is one who sees personality growth and responsible interaction as having an intrinsic place in the process of academic learning. Master teachers and learners no doubt long ago acquired the arts and skills of personalizing, expanding, and humanizing the teaching-learning experience far beyond the printed page. Adjunct to this doctrine is the educational existentialist who aims to educate people, not minds. This spirit in teaching-learning insists that observing, communicating and understanding are deficient without the ingredient of being a self; that learning without such involvement and self-awareness tends to deny existence. According to this, the biology professor/person teaches better than the biology professor.

The School as Fertile Soil for TCI

With teaching and learning as old as the beginning of mankind itself, it is sorrowful that the process of educating and being educated in school is under attack — much of it justified — from many directions. At this late date the teacher apparently still needs to master practical steps to bring meaning to the classroom so that students can "learn how to learn" (Postman and Weingartner, 1969). Yet it is only in the last few seconds of man's history that we find such concentrated attention being paid to feeling and interaction — modes that would obviously be a vital part of instruction.

For Rogers (1970) a good education would have at least some of the ingredients of an intensive group experience which serves as "an avenue to personal fulfillment and growth." As a result of such facilitation through encountering group experience, the individual could proceed as the initiator and protagonist of his own learning. The individual will become more personally involved and will permit the learning to affect him in many ways; he will become more active in evaluating the meaning of the learning for himself.

The comprehensive account of classroom teaching-learning closest to our approach is that of Jones (1968), who states, "the teacher's best course is . . . to bring the behavior in question into relevant commerce with . . . the subject matter. She has [thereby] increased the likeliness that personal development and academic development will come to synchronous terms." With Jones our aim — and indeed our method — is to coordinate developmental, cognitive, imaginal, and interactional skills with curriculum as much as possible. In this respect we build on the more piecemeal effort of "affective educators," like Alschuler (1970), who have developed courses and experiences leading to achievement motivation, creativity, awareness, and here-and-now living.

We also build on the findings of group dynamicists in their classroom applications. A review of our table page 43 reveals how the student can benefit when forces such as group norms, group goals, and leadership form a favorable climate for learning. The T-Group trainer (Miles, 1964), in addition to his insights about the classroom as a miniature social system, has other suggestions to make to the teacher. Teachers can benefit from the more rigorous model of the trainer who makes a "tentative intervention, studies its effect, diagnoses and intervenes again." The trainer's willingness to maximize attention to individuals, such as providing the learner with feedback, is also worthy of emulating. Neglected, but of great importance, is the T-Group trainer's offering of the subject matter of human relations itself as a contribution to the educational curriculum.

It is both the TCI group worker's approach and the teacher's dream to structure, to monitor, and to bring all the pragmatic benefits that are fitting to a given subject within the grasp of the participants. The school as a place for living-learning is indeed fertile soil for the development of TCI approaches.

Personal Freedom with Responsibility and Intellectual Rigor

While a more organized and thorough approach to TCI teaching-learning must await the preparation of further manuals and books, we attempt to spell out here at least the ABC of how it works. At first, a theme is articulated, based on the curriculum itself. The pupils state their relationship to and concern with the theme. Others in the group react, act, and interact to the content of what is being said as well as to the person and the way he has communicated. Thus every communication or event in class is experienced more richly by the participants who are trained to sense and perceive things at these different levels. Since so much of what emerges can be related by teacher and pupils to the theme at hand, flexibility and openness are generated with the resulting release of productive energy.

In a class discussion in history dealing with immigration, the statement was made by a student that he noticed "blacks are getting arrogant." In the ensuing period the teacher kept a three-way balance. The reality or content level was employed when the logic, definition, and validity of such a remark were discussed. Second was the meaning of such a phrase for the person who said it. Third was the impact on the listeners and their subsequent interactions. The spinning out of all of these interrelated threads created a fabric of shared learning and growth enlivened by the active and pleasurable involvement of an unusually high percentage of participants.

In earlier experiments to adapt TCI approaches to teaching, we witnessed the impact of the classroom setting on the TCI approach. This awareness of the "globe" or "ground" obliged us to make minor modifications in the method. It can no longer be assumed, as in TCI workshops, that everyone will cooperate. The teacher becomes the *chairman of the group* to fulfill a given segment of the curriculum — in a stronger sense than we do in a theme-centered interactional workshop, where, as we have said, the leader is the chairman of himself and the method. The TCI teacher retains his central position as specialist with the content and as transmitter of knowledge. He is appointed by school, society, parents, and students to take an evaluational role which he alone can do best. Can he be this kind of judge while trying to encourage spontaneous and committed learning? We think so, provided that the marks and ratings are mutually arrived at, are chiefly of a qualitative, descriptive character, and are part of a process of accepting and giving constructive criticism.

We also noticed a new form of "resistance" to TCI participation, based upon difficulties participants were having in balancing their affective, thinking, and interactive involvement. Those who had difficulties in emotional control complained that we were too much like the other "over-intellectualized" conventional classes; the constricted student with difficulty in letting go lamented over the "crap" that was going on to the detriment of learning; the fearful and shy students murmured to us after class that they didn't come here to interact in an "encounter group." The reason we term this "resistance" (with the implication of an unrealistic perception) is because we noticed that the complaints were made by the same class members who were finding it difficult to share their inner selves with the others in the process of learning. Secondly, these complaints were not in accord with what most of the participants felt to be happening at the time the complaints were made.

All we have said previously about the definition and benefits of a theme pertains to its use in the classroom. But here we must be prepared to deal with the "multiple" or "personal" theme aspect. Join a TCI workshop and you pursue a theme which declares the group's focus in a clear, simple, inviting way. But in the classroom, as well as in your family, you have an extended life situation where others and yourself have both tangible and more subtle built-in purposes — all throbbing concurrently. This is a factory with multiple products, people, and purposes, not an artist's studio with its single-hued theme of expressing creativity. You are enveloped by a score of themes.

Back in the classroom, the TCI social studies (or social science) instructor has the explicit theme "Experiential Involvement with Social Organizations" already agreed upon by the group. This is the group's focus. Concurrently the teacher has become convinced that in this group at this time his chief underlying theme — only partially shared with the others informally — is "Appreciating Differences in this Classroom." An accompanying peripheral theme (also partly shared with others) for Mary Ann is "Finding My Place in this Classroom." She at the moment is shaking out a blackboard eraser rather frantically.

This state leads to a hunt for typically useful personal or underlying themes which may be conveniently stored for immediate use by teacher and students. These themes are *not* distractions in our definition; rather they represent the multilevel and complex nature of a person's approach to any situation in life. No doubt, the most penetrating of these implicit themes is "Competing and Cooperating in Learning." This theme begins in nursery school and ends for some in a post-doctoral institution. The desirable condition of teacher-learner symmetry is served by the underlying themes of "Being Myself and Being a Teacher; Being Myself and Being a Learner." What teacher does not think of avoiding the educational approach in which life becomes congealed in textbooks and is then only partially thawed out in the classroom for practical application? The implicit theme here would be "Using Life as Source Material and Books as Tools." As to the social learning environment, the TCI teacher has a special stake in the kinds and quality of classroom friendships. Where a dyad is formed, this teacher strives not to have it exclude others from joining, modifying, and even challenging the output of the original group of two. The theme here would be "Letting Myself Be Known and Getting to Know Others." Most teachers today striving in the common cause of building our democracy have the ceaseless theme of "Identifying and Resisting Totalitarian Threats in the Dynamics of this Classroom."

As for explicit themes, we believe that there is frequent opportunity provided by the curriculum of any class. Granted, a class in Mandarin Chinese for high school seniors in Chicago provides more of an occasion for drilling in strange sounds and developing automatic responses. But why not an occasional ascent from the mines of skill building to the level of an experiential workshop session in "Personal Approaches to Hearing and Reproducing Unusual Sounds?"

Finally we have the whole range of explicit themes central to a wide range of curricula. These include a vast array of subject matter, issues, values, and personal as well as interpersonal concerns. The social sciences fit hand in glove with TCI learning-teaching because of the myriad connections possible with feelings, here-and-now interactions, and indeed the whole life of the participant.

The Learning-Teaching Code

We have devised a "learning-teaching code" based on the familiar TCI ground rules.[1] In its present form, this code is not meant as a manual for classroom participants but rather for the teacher who would interpret its provisions to her particular class in her own way.

TCI Ground Rule
Be your own chairman. Decide what you want to do.

TCI Learning-Teaching Code

1. With the help of others each learner identifies his own shifting levels of interest and participation in the theme.

Resistive — "In my present state in this setting I do not want to learn this material with these others."

Exploratory — "I will find out what I want to know. I will decide what to do with it."

Expediting — "I will start doing it. I will see if it works out as planned."

Experiential — "I will be involved in the learning experience as fully as I can."

---

[1]Gendlin's "ground rules for experiential groups" provided a few suggestive phrases for our formulation of the "learning-teaching code."

Experimental — "I will be free to learn in different ways using new and riskier approaches."

Evaluational — "I will look at myself and judge my efforts and results not harshly but not too leniently."

2. If you are here, you belong here. Be the guardian of your own words and actions. Listen carefully to what the other person is communicating.

TCI Ground Rule
Give to this situation what you want to give and to get from it.

TCI Learning-Teaching Code

Individual differences are respected by the teacher and each participant in giving and getting. Each person's living inside himself must be respected and gotten to, thereby enriching the person's awareness and the group's resources.

TCI Ground Rule
Disturbances and passionate involvements take precedence over the stated theme in order to be resolved.

TCI Learning-Teaching Code

In a classroom distractions will be frequently related to the person's approach to and withdrawal from learning. Other distractions such as joy, sorrow, and preoccupations with ongoing vicissitudes are not directly related to the learning process but to life. One of the most powerful aids to learning and teaching is the emphasis on bringing forth these distractions to help the wandering person back to the waiting group.

Side conversations, an apparent form of distraction, also take precedence. A whispered, furtive comment to a neighbor is often one's own association to the theme which could be of importance to others in the group. By hiding his side comments from the leader and others, the whisperer is reducing his chances to practice taking risks and to measure his intellectual output.

TCI Ground Rule

Speak for "I" and not for "We."

TCI Learning-Teaching Code

Take risks in intellectual self-statements. Do not use other authorities in the field or a vague assumption about a general "we" to mask your own reluctance or anxiety about identifying your thought processes. Take responsibility for your own viewpoint.

TCI Ground Rule

Make as many statements as possible and ask only important questions.

TCI Learning-Teaching Code

1) Be less dependent as a learner.

2) Be less evasive as a learner.

3) Be more self-actualizing as a learner.

This has been a description of our conservative attitude in improving education using a relevant approach to the contemporary educational malaise. Stress has been on the unity of cognitive *and* affective learning-teaching. We hope to point a way to make lives better *while* learning and teaching as functioning organisms.

XII

A
Therapeutic
Catalyst

The theme-centered interactional method was five years old before its practitioners started to apply it to counseling and therapy[1]. Those who had practiced group therapy in the morning and had participated in the Workshop Institute for Living-Learning at night had managed to keep these two procedures as separate as day and night.

---

[1]As we do not make a categorical distinction between these two terms, future references to TCI counseling have as their referent both counseling and psychotherapy.

Theoretical Dilemmas

Unraveling and resolving pathology or maladaptation was not at first clearly seen to be within the ken of a "workshop method." The focus was on giving recognition to and strengthening the positive and visible manifestations of personality. There was an assumed contradiction in workshop and therapy themes. The former was usually stated in positive, striving terms; the latter continued to be conceptualized in terms of personal problems. The unduly stringent separation of the pathology-health continuum conceptualized the counseling therapy office as a laboratory for fighting sickness on one hand, and made the workshop an inappropriate place for touching on psychodynamics or alleviating emotional difficulty on the other.

The assumed irreconcilability of the analytic and experiential was also based on the practice that the analytic therapist acts neutrally, while the experiential therapist or group leader is personally open and freely interactive with patients. In this genre of group therapy, *analysis* of process was becoming anathema; even reflective comment on interpersonal events with psychological distance was sometimes frowned upon. This quasi-nihilistic attitude toward "thinking about what we are doing" exerted force on the direction of group therapy. It constituted — on the positive side of the ledger — a challenge to other long-term forms of treatment where insights lack application, transference persists opaquely, and experiential change is virtually absent in the daily life of the patient. But unfortunately, former persistent emphasis on understanding self and others for the sake of improving interaction now gave way to gut-feelings which tended to loom larger than life.

There is now a felt need to enhance the whole person and foster therapy which can synthesize the ego more naturally. One example of this desire is the emergence of theme-centered interactional counseling and therapy. Here the leader and group choose specific themes for work- and play-like experimentation. In an atmosphere of heightened awareness, consciousness is expanded as each person relates himself to some meaningful facet of the human problems of those present. The experiential is emphasized as a way to make behavior more socially fitting and personally fulfilling. At the same time, the counselor retains and creatively applies his knowledge of psychodynamics and group process.

Certain questions and answers frequently dealt with by trainees in the TCI method assist the reader to achieve a better grasp of his functioning as a TCI counselor.

1. Can the TCI counselor be both himself, experientially, as well as the neutral figure who invites projections?

The counselor is seen as both authority and peer, whether he plans to be or not. Both distorted and consensually valid perceptions of him are in evidence. With respect to his actual function as an expert, he embraces the experience and shares at times his feelings about it. With regard to transferences, he opens the door wide enough to admit the transference which is germane to a working out of the theme. He plays host to certain transferential reactions and chooses not to foster others which would deflect the theme from center. For example, there was a post-summer counseling group for regional assistant scout leaders with the theme of "Keeping Down Hang-Ups." The counselor planfully took in stride the hypercritical remarks of Member J. At a point the counselor intervened and worked on the transference relationship. It turned out that J's fear of a threatening, scrutinizing parent had been so pronounced that his resulting defensiveness had made it impossible for him even to begin to view his own difficulties with younger boys.

2. Can the TCI counselor encourage production from both past and present — as well as future — without violating the experiential approach?

The TCI counselor does not disassociate the past and future from the present, since he sees the theme as a continuum which spontaneously selects the time segment which is most alive at any given moment. There is a built-in timelessness to the theme. How-ever, the recurring focus is usually the present because it is in this tense that interaction is most authentic. The cognitive brought in from the past — in the form of vivid knowledge of a subject — is obviously valued and can be used to enlarge the range of shared experience. There is added reason to respect past and future. The TCI counselor, aiming for behavioral change, is interested in every element of biography invoked by the theme. He recognizes that change can be facilitated where clarifying connections are made between the present and past and the present and future.

3. How can the leader, an expert on psychodynamics and personality organization, actively intervene in terms of behavioral modification if as a TCI counselor he is supposed to function more

subjectively as "his own chairman"?

The TCI counselor functions as scientist and artist. As a scientist, he relates understanding and modifies normal and pathological behavior process. He serves concurrently as an artist by dint of fitting his treatment plan into the given experiential matrix and making his interventions with sensibility and finesse.

4. If the TCI view of living-learning is one where potential is used to override pathology, why and how is pathology dealt with directly?

Here the counselor's procedure closely matches that of the conventional group therapist. Manifestations of pathology, such as excessive anxiety, breakdown of defenses, and gross parataxic distortions, can be confronted and, if possible, analyzed and resolved. At the same time he employs a positive, supportive attitude where he senses the appropriate moment for building strengths by using the client's and patient's healthier reserves.

5. What forms of unconscious behavior are reachable by and tractable to TCI counseling?

All known forms of unconscious behavior may be approached in a TCI therapeutic milieu. Of course, the counselor accepts the ethical injunction which requires that he perform at the level of competence and experience which his training and supervision justify.

6. If child and latency groups do best with play and activity, how can TCI counseling be at all useful with these ages?

Play and activity modalities are included in those approaches which can be adapted for the TCI method. There are verbal and nonverbal themes in activity and play which are as viable as the themes of a sophisticated group of executives. To discern and deal with these themes (verbally or not) requires the skill of a specialist in treating children, adept at understanding and translating the symbolic meaning of play into everyday language and its thematic equivalent.

An Outline of Structure and Procedure

The following table summarizes the main features of TCI counseling.

TABLE 12

Theme-Centered Interactional Counseling (and Psychotherapy)

1. *Definition*	A harnessing of therapeutic and experiential approaches in a helping relationship.
2. *Theoretical Basis*	Involvement in exploring a theme to make it easier for the individual to express and experience problems; experiments with ways of relating. Release of bound, fixated energy through a growing acceptance of each person's physical, emotional, and intellectual enjoyment in the here and now; relating interpersonally with a shared theme.
3. *Referral*	Self, parents, teachers, agencies.
4. *Aims — Benefits*	Aims: the same as those in basic group counseling and group therapy (re-educative, reconstructive), with emphasis on development of health-ful resources particular to each individual. Benefits: a) functional homo-geneity of membership enhanced through a shared thematic field; b) the cognitive made more assimilable by involved participants; c) the theme, introduced by the design of the leader, which is therefore better timed and more relevantly formulated than it would have been if completely left to chance.
5. *Duration and Composition*	Six to twelve in a group. Five to fifty sessions; one and a half hours or more each session. Closed group. Homogeneous or heterogeneous.

6. *Ground Rules*   (Counseling and Psychotherapy) Free speech, aiming at openness, intuition, and empathy. (Theme-Centered) Involvement to promote autonomous and interdependent functioning as detailed in Chapter VI.

7. *Content*   History, current environmental problems, intra-group reactions, personal feelings, perceptions, sensations, with focusing by counselor on personal-social adjustment, defense mechanisms, conflicts, growing up, and school learning. Examples of theme areas: exploring social issues in depth, expediting new moments of personal growth, working with soluble dilemmas, experimenting with new ways of living.

8. *Special Nature of Experience*   Sharpening, focusing, and activating the content of a therapeutic session.

9. *Stages — Sequences*   Initial (reconnaissance, rapport), middle (working through), and ending phases (separation, evaluation). Use of one or more specific "modes" (see Chapter VIII) to help to define stages-sequences with greater clarity of overall process and purpose.

10. *Leader*   Plays an advanced role in self-actualizing. Balances the I (self), We (group interaction), and It (theme).

11. *Member*   Defers to the positive tone which the experience fosters; lets relationships develop in the course of making the theme his reality.

12. *Motivation —Resistance*

Motivation high if anxiety and pain pronounced. Recurrent resistance because of stress of change. However, enhancement of motivation and reduction of anxiety possible due to "forward motion" and sense of accomplishing of the theme-centered approach.

13. *Transferences —Realities*

Transference minimized, as the syntaxic mode is favored with respect to the theme, the others, the leader, and the self.

14. *Uniqueness*

Grist for the mill of members' and leaders' ingenuity in solving relevant problems provided by the integration of the therapeutic and workshop approaches.

Beginnings in a TCI Counseling Group

Schools, agencies, clinics, or private offices are typical settings for such groups. The referred client or patient has already received an evaluation or individual therapy and, feeling the need for more counseling or therapy in a social setting, is seen individually by the TCI leader. Further confirmation of his readiness to enter a group is established, and questions are answered regarding the group in general, schedules, fears, and expectations. Primary ground rules about confidentiality, speaking for oneself, and airing distractions are given briefly. Examples of themes which may arise are offered. The client is asked to suggest a theme most pertinent to himself. He is told that theme shifts and develops as a result of group discussion and interaction and that the theme at any given time will be relevant to and instrumental in helping him.

Entering the group, the client finds others openly sharing their stubborn pathology to rid themselves of problems. The leader and group have selected a theme which provides a compelling center of focus for his thinking, feeling, and interacting. In this way the patient's energies are marshalled in experiencing and discovering more about himself and others.

In many forms of group therapy life is held in abeyance in a sense, while the patients deal with such things as defense mechanisms, history, resistances, patterns of neurotic behavior, and regressive and self-defeating realities of the person. In TCI counseling and therapy these realities are not neglected but are viewed in the context of one's becoming more productive and gratifying. If a group were to include instructors and students from various colleges, with participants presenting anxieties and frustrations as teachers and learners, an initial theme, "Building an Authentic College Community," could be crystallized and pursued for several sessions. The involved participant would be reminded of and confronted with his own obstacles and strengths in the learning-teaching milieu of college and TCI group.

The growth and "full humanness" orientation of TCI counseling (Gordon and Liberman, 1971) is clearly revealed as the participants are invited to share their healthier potentials, thereby "getting on top of" the pathology without camouflaging it. Through the theme this method aims at eliciting those facets of behavior and experience which are most timely for relevant therapy. It happened that in a high school therapy group the presenting problems were associated with apathy and detachment in learning. The leader constructed the theme of "Freeing Ingenuity in Learning," thereby supplying a theme-centered occasion in which group members were guided experientially to constructive and creative alternatives.

TCI counseling, with its predeliction for seeing individual behavior and experience in the light of themes, may be more attuned to the relationship between the client's problems and contemporary issues. Once, in an early session of a college counseling group the theme-centered counselor became aware of the connections between personal growth problems and the choices for various identification models. His proposed theme of "Hippies, Squares, Radicals, and I" served as the central point of interaction and personal reflection. As encounter became more authentic, personality difficulties and dynamics emerged.

Tailoring the Treatment Plan

Those who seek "group experiences," such as working together or relating to a variety of other people, are challenged and fulfilled by the steady unfolding of various group events including impasses, frustrations, defections, destructive liaisons. Providing this experience readily is a "leaderless group" or a group leader who follows the mystique that whatever he or the group does may somehow "click" for most members. When, however, a therapeutically oriented group leader is strongly committed to working adaptively and selectively with individuals in a group, he starts with a "treatment plan." This beginning blueprint — modified as the group and members make progress — is the therapist's formulation of the person developmentally, dynamically, and etiologically in the context of specific goals within a particular group setting. The experienced group therapist has a treatment plan with essential and fitting parts. A psychoanalytically oriented treatment plan of a group therapist[1] might be condensed in this way:

The *history* of a thirty-year old woman reveals a lifetime of fear of women. Mother is childish and a nag; father was nice, at times too seductive; he died when she was a teen-

---

[1]Dr. Alexander Wolf has provided some of these specific formulations.

ager. Patient has son and daughter. Husband is a musician. Work brings him together with young singers.

Symptoms: anxiety reactions, phobias about broken toys, separation fears, and seeing husband as if he were father.

Diagnosis: obsessive-compulsive, anxiety reactions. (Ego strength and relatedness to others adequate for the uncovering of analytic group therapy.)

Dynamics: Patient's fear of abandonment —seen in obsessive jealousy toward female singers — related to getting punished for incestuous wishes generated by relationship with father. Underlying homosexual feelings toward girl singers and own daughter related to inability to assume adult female role.

Working through in the group: exposing, experiencing, and resolving the *core problem* at various levels. Here the Freudian formulation of the core problem is that the patient is still preoccupied with displacing infantile mother. Adopting mother's childish ways, patient hopes to win father. When patient "assists" group therapist as a little girl, this effort is seen as effort to get to father by "creeping into mother's skin." In relationship to a male group member, patient experiences her childish pretenses and relates this experience to relationship with husband.

Goals (patient): getting relief from feelings of hostility and jealousy and developing secure feelings as wife and mother.

Goals (group therapist): resolve patient's parental transferences; reinforce her adaptive behavior. Autonomy and interdependence as goals intrinsic to this and every therapeutic interactional experience.

With parallel but not as intensive training, the group counselor or social group worker in a therapeutic role is unprepared to enter into full use of all the therapeutic tools. But consider a few rich, creative applications from the mine of group therapy sources. The counselor could apply a "counseling plan" based upon developmental tasks related to the pupils in his group and formulate an appropriate theme. Or the social group worker (who is using a TCI therapeutic approach) with her knowledge of family relationships could make a plan for a pre-adolescent aimed at a nonthreatening airing of his family relationships. The context here would be activity group therapy with a theme of "Working and Playing in My Family."

The TCI treatment plan, incorporating elements from group therapy treatment planning, is a useful guide to the quality and limits of the leader's interventions. By first evaluating the patient psychodynamically, this TCI group leader evaluates the individual in terms of his ability to balance self and group and task effectively. In what vector does the patient need most encouragement to participate and grow? In a session with the theme "Removing Barriers between People," one member in a group devoted to an expediting mode was stiffly conveying his own personal associations. In relation to the theme, he was stressing the "I." Here the group leader's plan was to press for more fantasy material of any sort before encouraging a more direct interaction. This emphasis served as a useful step in building ego strength for that individual in an interpersonal-thematic moment. A second step followed in stressing the "I" but leaning toward the "We." The client was encouraged to give his intuitions about what others in the group were feeling. Several sessions later, the leader encouraged actual confrontations between this client and significant others in the group. According to the treatment plan, this client was now ready to work through the theme with more mature interaction.

The plan for others differed according to their psychodynamics. At times, the "We" (interaction) was encouraged through encountering; for another client the "It" (the cognitive, the task) was stressed to help clarify thinking and develop personal values.

As implied in Chapter VIII, the mode of participation can be assigned an important part in a TCI treatment plan. Engaging the person and finding that pathway which would optimally release energy, improve balance, and bring into play new and exciting facets of personality, the TCI counselor may use mode to great advantage. If, the conventional group counselor finds himself in a problem-solving, reality-testing phase (expediting) or in a free-swinging experiential vein, he may be responding to an opportunity for therapy, not calling it "mode." But it is unlikely that he would either press the use of mode to its fullest or that, conceptualizing this as an ongoing process, he would institute a series of sessions based on a mode. The TCI counselor has the benefit of viewing his work through conceptual prisms which have the five modes set in their time and place, permitting him to shift easily and skillfully from one mode to the next.

Working with significant modes of action by group members, the TCI counselor-therapist conceptualizes life as a productive task, socially meaningful and pleasurably experienced. Let us review briefly, for example, the first three modes of action:

1) *Exploratory.* Enhancing self-awareness; bringing into being a map which structures social experience; finding how to explore a task best.
2) *Expediting.* Accepting the task of self-improvement and working it through; choosing a complex task and completing its performance.
3) *Experiential.* Relating fully to others and oneself to achieve authenticity and integration.

These modes of behavior in group counseling enable the client to move in closer touch with his own impulses, his conscience, and his ego. While these modes of behavior are rooted in the image of man as a healthy maker of life, at the same time they respect and work with the manifestations of conflict, anxiety, and disruption in personality organization. These modes also provide a focus on the here-and-now, task-oriented goals both within and outside the group. Thus the goal (part of the treatment plan) in the group for an immature, anxious, hysterical man would be for him to accept the role of a committed, thinking participant who takes responsibility for the pace and direction of the session. The "mode of action" for this patient might be "expediting," which would at the same time serve to counterbalance his tendency to be excessively labile.

The Central Position of the Theme

The theme, ever in focus, has an underlying importance in the structure and flow of treatment. While pervading moods and content with a common denominator are often used by conventional group counselors and therapists as a rallying point, the TCI counselor is more finely attuned to the formation and utilization of themes and their value to specific individuals in the group. Well-selected themes will waken the most significant and changeable patterns of personality in the individual. A young man of fourteen who was brash and provocative in groups was unable to modify his self-defeating pattern when the leader dealt directly with exhibitionism as the patient's means of surpassing a rejecting father. This same leader had occasion to convert this group to a TCI format. With the theme of "Getting Recognition for My Achievements," a graceful and workable approach successfully engaged the same adolescent within an experiential theme related to the actual movement and unfolding of his life. In this instance the theme made a significant contribution to the treatment plan. In the leader's first effort, while the psycho-dynamic formulation was undoubtedly correct, the boy seemed to be able to make only limited use of it.

The use of theme is fruitful in therapeutic groups, as it takes the individual's problems and converts them into the currency of a shared problem. This benefit of course is the same as the widely stated advantage of homogenous groups (mothers with problems, students with speech problems, and so forth). But the comparison stops there. In TCI therapeutic groups the themes are kept in focus because they are part and parcel of a principle of the TCI approach to process and content: "theme-centering."

The question has been raised, "If a theme by definition has a positive, striving message, how can a problem theme be adequately expressed?" Even in TCI counseling we practice framing the theme in positive terms; we see the will as a positive thing — in Rank's and Maslow's terms. Accordingly, the theme is designed to evoke an active response of thought, feeling, and movement. When people enter a group for the purpose of dealing with pathology, their response to a positively-stated theme becomes freely loaded with problem content, thus becoming available to correctively oriented interventions.

As the theme establishes its early and permanent place in the life and process of the group, members enjoy the challenge of moving together from their present position toward a shared goal. This process calls for cooperation and releases productive energy. It serves to diminish alienation because the group member sees his problem not merely as "something others have too" but as one in-stance of a general theme. The client often feels something like this: "I talked about my problem-theme in those terms which made sense to me and which were adapted from other people's productions while living a shared, intense experience of thinking, feeling, and interaction." In a young adult TCI counseling group, several themes crystallized over a period of months. Several members were pre-occupied with dissolving marriages and engagements. The ensuing theme was established: "Letting Go of Situations and Seeing New Relationships." By working through this theme (for this group in an experiential mode), attention became centered on interreligious friendships, the clash of value systems, and age gaps with the TCI counselor. "Bridging and Benefiting from Differences" thus became the agreed-upon theme, continuing for two more sessions.

It should be noted that the pre-selection or evolution of a theme by leader and group will not have the effect of constraining the participant from bringing up problems of his or her own. Each person tends to interpret the theme in keeping with what pleases or bothers him the most. The well-tempered theme has a valence for penetrating a wide range of personality disorders. It has also been observed that some who do not acquiesce to a given theme at first are unexpectedly drawn into and greatly helped by this treatment.

Promoting Disturbances

Disturbances have been referred to in the TCI ground rules as omnipresent distractions from the theme, regularly experienced by every group participant and leader. It is typical to hear someone saying, "I've just become very tense around my knees, and I cannot hear what is being said," or "I can't stop thinking about what my friend told me this morning about his plan to take a flying lesson next weekend." We wish to make clear how by expressing and resolving disturbances in a group, bound-up energy can be released for work and interaction. The apparent loss of efficiency in dealing with disturbances is to be seen as a tactical loss but a strategic gain.

While the term "resistance" in therapy is most applicable to the therapeutic experience, the concept of disturbance could be gainfully employed both in TCI therapeutic groups and in its basic educational workshop form. Freud's discovery of resistance enabled the patient to make contact with what his unconscious was saying about his changing and about those people associated with his changing and getting better. Cohn's concept of disturbance in a group facilitated the work of TCI-oriented groups in broader and, in a sense, new directions. In our view disturbance may be seen in two forms: one is the kind of inner distraction or intrapsychic event which may not be connected with ongoing group process; second is thought, feeling, or behavior which is more manifestly related to the ongoing event.

If theme serves as a fixed point of reference, disturbance counterbalances whatever inherent rigid effect the theme may have. By raising his dissonant voice in passing, the group member helps to invite change in the group's purpose; the group may then subscribe to it. He may have a novel idea or an overlooked approach which the group can adopt. These interruptions serve to cut down the operant and rigid fiction of group life: that an announced task will be permanently accepted. The use of disturbances gives recognition to the fact that, as in a well-functioning marriage, the unfolding group experience changes the structure of membership and influences the themes. On the other hand, it will be recalled that resistance in groups is confined to the preoccupation of a patient more with his own associations than with an objective statement about the theme, himself, and others. Thus a TCI disturbance is not conceptualized as a hindrance to productive action. At the same time, the leader tries to avoid having this temporarily deviant behavior become an exercise in self-preoccupation. The focus is group effectiveness and bringing the person back to the group rather than supplying an occasion for multiplying catharsis and improving mental health — as is the case in group therapy.

We illustrate the benefit of using disturbance to broaden and make more flexible a set theme:

In a suburban school district a large percentage of the counselors had developed their professional skills on the job but had not had the benefit of personal therapy experiences as had some of their younger colleagues. Their work with clients suffered because they could not empathize with those in "the other chair." They were receptive to the theme of "Myself and Client" in the framework of a TCI counseling group with an experimental mode. Bella, a woman in her early fifties, took a seat a short distance from the others and became detached from the group. Encouraged to state her distractions, she said, "I have had many experiences of receiving help which could not be labeled therapeutic in a formal sense. I feel frustrated because I cannot relate these pertinent experiences to a group where the theme is to bring oneself in here as a client." Another woman immediately recalled a forgotten experience in which she had received remarkable relief from an informal talk with an uncle. Another group member quickly commented, "I would like to see an addition to the theme, making it "Myself as a Client and a Recipient of Help." This suggestion was zestfully accepted by the others.

If a person is routinely unable to deal satisfactorily with his disturbance — as sometimes may be true in everyday life — we find the ill effects of suppression and repression. We begin to see how energy is stolen from the actions and purposes of its victim as an aftereffect of camouflaging, acting out, or self-concealment. In the TCI model, since disturbances take precedence, there is a greater chance that the person will attempt to throw off his encumbrance. The group is a helpful setting; the leader may ask him, "Who in this room can help you over this fatigue?" or "What can you say or do now to feel better?" The benefits to the individual, aside from the general releasing effect, may now be stated specifically.

(1) His relation to the group is reactivated, and his preoccupation with himself can now be traded in for increased interest in the theme.

(2) By taking responsibility for his distraction, the group member finds it easier to bring it under control and bring himself back to the theme.

(3) This is as good or better an occasion than any other to become better known by other members, thereby strengthening the feeling of being a participant.

(4) The paradigmatic effect of having others go along with and ride out the disturbance provides him with a more realistic image of himself by way of this feedback. It then relieves him of the disturbance by way of becoming more self-aware and theme-centered with renewed authenticity.

XIII

Living-Learning

Nourished by individual counseling theory and by the rich and varied sources of group approaches, the theme-centered interactional system has a special identity of its own. In examining those taproots referred to in Chapters I-IV, we wish to trace their junctions with the TCI approach. Thus we have also an opportunity to sketch the broader outlines and conclusions relative to TCI theory and practice.

Incorporating the Essence and Uniqueness of Counseling

Theme-centered interactional theory and practice is centered on the person fulfilling a task. The TCI model participant has succeeded in learning and growing in relation to a central theme. The cognitive material or *content* stands for the perceivable and malleable world. This learning and growing is underscored by counseling theorists who stressed content. Without this element, the group member may become conscious of physical sensation, strong emotion, or group atmosphere, but he will not be relating these experiences to particular tasks or themes in life.

The job of advising and guiding has often been devalued as superficial and unimportant, even the cause of excessive dependency. The early exponents of content in counseling made a useful contribution as they were already aware of the existence and motivating power of themes in every human transaction.

The TCI approach, building on such content, carries this emphasis one step further by a more sensitive formulation and working through of theme in the group. By way of its articulation, this TCI theme is also adapted to dealing with questions intimately related to life rather than more formal, dry subject matter. In learning to pursue this kind of theme better, the participant learns to make his life better because group life and extra-group life are blended.

The inner and outer transactions which go on between people are so complex that a wide variety of theories of *process* have been adopted by counselors. There is yet no description of TCI interpersonal process which can match the subtleties and intricacies of the psychoanalytic or existential.

In Chapter X we began to expand descriptions of TCI process. What TCI theory does offer in a general sense of process is the emphasis upon the interrelationship between thought, feeling, and behavior. We say that what the group member gives or takes at a given moment is a resultant of his relationship to the theme and to the others in the group. As do counseling theorists, we also stress ways of freeing associations between one person and the next. Our specific ways are through setting a positive atmosphere and using the ground rules and the example of a leader serving as an authentic self to accomplish this end.

Counseling theory, dealing as often as it did with children and adolescents in stages of mastering developmental tasks, contributed to an understanding of normal *human development.* In the TCI approach we work with every individual in any tense he selects — past, present, future. This is our means of bringing out awareness of genetic and developmental factors. The developmental focus in counseling theory also provided us with the background of facts about human development — particularly in schools and colleges — contrib ʿ: ng appropriate themes pertinent to a given level. The TCI approach has also derived from guidance and counseling theory a familiarity with the concept of educational development as related to overall personal development. Through TCI we may build on the tradition which values the goal of balanced human development in both process and product.

When psychotherapy strayed too far from the presenting level of problems, when it became too removed from real people solving real problems, the counselor maintained a balance by using himself as a tool. He held to the conviction that helping the client to become more aware is most effective when balanced with his own pursuit of being a self-actualizing individual. At the same time he tended to avoid the two extremes in using himself: on the one hand, an authoritarian direction-giver; on the other, a person more thoroughly involved in just being than committed to doing his work.

In the same way, the TCI leader has aimed for the most fitting mean between the "objective" and "subjective" roles. He sees his task as both being the guardian of the method ("making it happen") and being the more free-flowing, interactive, authentic chairman of himself ("letting it happen").

The central ideals of the counselor have been to *combine and integrate* whatever modalities fit a particular situation, person, or group. Those who have experimented with the theory and application of the TCI method have also searched out schools of thought within counseling which, when combined with our own basic TCI structure, could contribute maximum results with the minimum of effort. It is therefore not at all surprising to find various TCI groups serving a spectrum of needs within a person, a school, a clinic, a community, an industry.

Augmenting Guidance, Counseling, and Therapy in Groups

As we view the march of guidance, counseling, and therapy in groups, we find ourselves at the focus of a major emergent. All of those efforts were bent to use the past and the here-and-now to open the way for each participant's shared interaction. The emergent to which we refer is the realization that the group must become both the instrument and the goal for the person's development; that it must provide a linkage between past, present, and future; that it must not be merely a way of recognizing problems or evoking strong feelings without the accompaniment of understanding.

We believe that it is the theme in a TCI group which fulfills these crucial purposes. In working through the theme, each member is (1) connected to one another through an ongoing process of thought, feeling, and behavior; (2) involved in what is now and in the immediate application of the now to his goal following the group experience. It is this binding quality of the theme which makes the TCI approach an emergent in living-learning from the established fields of guidance, counseling, and therapy in groups. Thus for Joe seeking an answer to career problems in group guidance, we offer to enliven his theme as its connections with himself and others become apparent. For Jane seeking relief from shyness in a counseling group, we provide the inviting and searching quality of related themes along with the experiential thrust of here-and-now interaction.

A Grounding for Experiential and Other Process Groups

The TCI approach may be viewed in the light of the recent "group explosion" which brought to life a number of new emphases and schools of thought — mostly along experiential lines. The common denominator is a turning toward humanistic conceptions of self-actualization. In Maslow's (1962) words, "This psychology is not purely descriptive or academic; it suggests action and implies con-sequences. It helps to generate a way of life, not only for the person himself within his own private psyche, but also for the same person as a social being, a member of society."

In our opinion there is an unfortunate overemphasis upon process in the experiential and encounter models. There is a turning away from the content of people's lives, past, present, and future. In this connection we note in these groups a tendency to predetermine and fashion specific interpersonal processes, while the intrapersonal is respectfully neglected. This is not to imply that the individual is neglected. Rather in process groups it is largely through the group that we measure the man. And the man is conceptualized in a molar way as having certain general qualities to a degree which may in turn be enhanced.

Even with certain assets and advantages the group process is frankly limited in its concept of what goes into a human experience. It apparently overemphasizes the cathartic. In addition, it is satisfied with *labelling* the tactics of human beings, failing to see each interaction as part of the larger strategy of human life.

As an emergent of experiential and process groups, the TCI approach provides a sort of grounding in its emphasis upon conserving the best of group work. It does this by avoiding the temptation of imbuing participants with a zeal to engage in "process," "experience," games, and devices per se. On the other hand, in the TCI way we employ these practices discretely and maintain caution as to their mob effects. We do not stress action, dialogue, body experiencing, or practical solutions for their own sake, particularly where there is a passive acquiescence to other members or the group leader. Rather we work for the modes and moods into which the individual can genuinely enter.

The exciting, yet confusing encounter movement needs a TCI grounding. We want to integrate without violating or denigrating. We want to liberate without going to formlessness. We seek to avoid spurious relationships. We aim to respect people's genuine wariness of groups which do not compel them to find pathways toward getting what they want. We abhor the use of group for controlling and totalitarian purposes.

Conclusions

General and Historical

1) A TCI group approach in answer to the dehumanizing crisis of our time builds in people and their communities learning and loving as alternatives to paralysis and panic. The emphasis on release of human potential links the TCI leader more readily to students, teachers, administrators, and others in the community.

2) We can reach and hold wider populations because of the relatively nonthreatening use of theme as opposed to those methods which probe for pathology.

3) The TCI participant engages in a life-balancing, common-sense, aesthetic, whole-person approach which eschews treating or training the person as a piece or part-process of something.

4) There are many avenues of approach open from leader to participant or from one member to the next. This openness promotes situations where we can break into or break up habitual patterns of responding so that new behavior can be developed.

5) The teacher, guidance counselor, and other group workers are burdened by disparate elements in role and function. The reconciliation of opposing or parallel issues — such as "knowing or being," "persuasion or letting" — is facilitated through the balancing process of TCI.

Eclectic and Integrative

1) TCI theory is characterized by its many connections with other approaches. It is intrinsically related to the *learning-teaching process.* It parallels education because of its flexibility in adjusting to the interplay of imagination, memory, fantasy, ideas, ideals, and values. Going beyond many of today's educational practices, it is more sensitive to the need for personal involvement in any facet of the teaching-learning process.

2) Parallel to *therapists,* TCI practitioners are interested in fostering spontaneity and respect for styles of individuals and styles of living. As in counseling and therapy, the goal is to clarify the dynamics of interpersonal behavior and to develop self-actualizing relationships. The TCI approach elicits those facets of behavior and experience which are most timely for relevant therapy in the here-and-now. It does "necessary therapy" rather than "programming" preconceived formulations, and it accents the discovering of healthy potential.

3) On *group-dynamic and group-process* occasions, it was discovered how to recognize, but not prevent, problems in group interaction. Leaders learned how to make people proficient in turning the lights on to these phenomena. In the TCI experience we avoid exciting participants with the idea of engaging in "process" per se. Rather we welcome these manifestations in a way designed to respect the complexity of multiple human encounter but to avoid making an aberration out of it.

Both in experiential and process-type groups as well as in TCI groups, the participants and leader foster the ideals of moment-to-moment authenticity in their work. Surpassing the experiential and encounter groups in providing structure, the TCI model supplies the means of guiding experience by a sense of purpose and sharpening experience by presenting it with theme-centered occasions.

4) The TCI leader who serves as *group consultant* aims to explore and clarify the real situation which needs changing by using cognitive and practical measures. In addition, he has the advantage of releasing the client's energies for identifying and resolving the problems through theme centering. Intellectual interpretation or tapping feelings can be selectively adapted according to the person's own response to the theme. In this sense, the participant signals his own need and style of learning and relating, and the TCI leader takes his cue from this signal.

Structure and Process

1) We have formulated constructs as well as the design for machinery to deal in a balanced and parsimonious way with complex phenomena. The *I-We-It* configuration provides a balance wheel for the workings of theme exploration. Energy flows back and forth from unused sources of inner and outer *awareness* to *consciousness* of specific and important aspects of the learning experience. The *mode* is a single channel for the flow of complex data which emerge in a TCI group. The leader (and more experienced group members) aim at *balancing* the cognitive, conative, and affective, one or the other of which has become overemphasized or neglected in some forms of group participation and in daily living. The accompanying *ground rules* provide the constitution for an autonomous and interdependent give and take.

2) Underlying the TCI counseling (and the TCI workshop) concept of human change is an account given by Ruth C. Cohn.[1] She suggests that human change is activated when we give recognition to any part of the personality which has previously not been experienced in a realistic way and when we stimulate growth where it has not taken place before. These include such diverse areas as physical tensions, emotional needs on a childhood level, limited and narrow perceptual fields, and developmental lags. Whenever such

[1]Personal communication.

recognition is integrated and accepted by the participant, this new event becomes an agent of health which is likely to spread through the whole personality.

3) The man, woman, and child in our culture are confronted by social and historical issues, all of which can fragment energies and confuse value systems. To sustain the unifying force of a person's wholeness and integrity, we advance the use of experiential themes, themselves a force for synthesizing that which has been shaken loose. Working with the theme in the ways we have mentioned, a person engages in the ego-strengthening tasks of reality testing and in the strengthening through practical group experience of neglected parts of his personal and interpersonal functioning.

4) Diagrammatically, each person in the TCI group is relating to

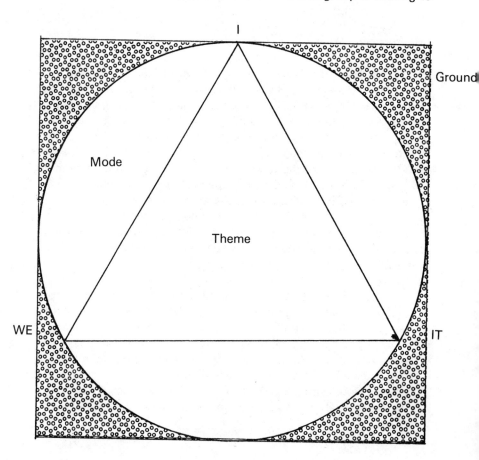

the theme in three ways: subjectively-affectively, cognitively, and interpersonally, with the theme providing a springboard. This structure is represented by the triangle[1] with the theme at center. The globe[2] surrounding the triangle is the mode or pathway which determines the flavor of the thrust in dealing with the task. Finally, no group effort would be realistic or serious without paying attention to the "culture" or setting of the event. This is the outer frame[3] or ground.

A Model of Person — A Model of Group

1) In the TCI workshop and therapeutic versions, our model for the individual is the "reasonable adventurer," the person of sensibility, the "congruent" and self-actualizing person, the participant who learns to lead himself. We aim to achieve this model not through focus on intrapsychic growth or interpersonal socializing experiences alone. We try to make it possible for healthy interaction to replace anxious interaction. We hope to have each dialogue or subgroup experience produce opportunities for even idiosyncrasies of personality to become special moments of I-thou communication about themes of shared relevance. The *living-learning* effect occurs as each member lets the relationship develop in the course of making the theme his reality.

2) The TCI philosophy takes into account the broader social issue of how individuals can enjoy the legitimate power of stating needs, intentions, and rugged individuality up to the point where their enactment infringes upon others. From the group side we are concerned with how members can assert their real needs for the devotion and support of others — but only to the degree where, in so doing, they will not cripple their selfhood.

3) The TCI group is most like the individuals who comprise it. It is not a perfectly functioning unit but can hope only to supply partial and even awkward solutions. The model group maintains its cohesiveness around the theme. This centripetal force helps the individual to concentrate on his purpose, along with the needs and desires of the others who are committed to the same theme. The positive mood of the group accompanies efforts to balance the learning experience in its I-We-It components. This is the setting in which

[1,2,3]This triangle, globe, and frame represent a slight variation from the globe and triangle pictured by the W.I.L.L. organization.

the dilemmas of group life can be worked through under favorable and more understandable conditions.

4) We see the TCI group not as task forced but as task centered, where the outcome cannot be assumed; we merely start with the willingness to work toward success. We are goal aware but not goal directed. In the agenda of ordinary groups you cannot talk of yourself as a free person for fear of being considered a deviant who somehow cannot contribute to the ongoing theme or task. In a TCI group, each person's style of work and contribution is not judged but rather seen in the context of how he can contribute to the theme.

Bibliography

Ackerman, N.W. *Treating the Troubled Family.* New York: Basic Books, 1966.

Alschuler, A.S. et al. *Teaching Achievement Motivation: Theory and Practice in Psychological Education.* Middletown, Conn.: Education Ventures, Inc., 1970.

Alexander, F. and French, T.M. *Psychoanalytic Therapy.* New York: Ronald Press Co., 1946.

Andrews, E.E. "Some Group Dynamics in Therapy Groups of Mothers." *International Journal of Group Psychotherapy* 12

(1962):476-492.

Arbuckle, D.S. "The Self of the Counselor." *Personal and Guidance Journal* 44 (1966):807-813.

Axline, Virginia. *Play Therapy.* New York: Houghton Mifflin, 1947.

Benne, K.D. "History of the T-Group in the Laboratory Setting." In *T-Group Theory and Laboratory Method,* edited by L.P. Bradford, et al., pp. 80-136. New York: John Wiley and Sons, Inc., 1964.

Bennett, Margaret E. *Guidance and Counseling in Groups.* New York: MGraw Hill, 1963.

Berdie, R.F. "Counseling: An Educational Technique." *Educational and Psychological Measurement* 9 (1949):89-94.

Berger, M.M. "Similarities and Differences between Group Psychotherapy and Intensive Short Term Group Process Experiences - Clinical Impressions." *The Journal of Group Psychoanalysis and Process* 1 (1968):11-31.

Bonney, W.C. "Pressures Toward Conformity in Group Counseling." *The Personnel and Guidance Journal* 43 (1965):970-973.

Bordin, E.S. *Psychological Counseling.* New York: Appleton-Century-Crofts, 1955.

Boris, H.N. *The (Un)Examined Life.* The College-School-Rural Community Mental Health Consultation Project. Plainfield, Vermont: N.I.M.H. Report OM 00062-67, 1967.

Boy, A.V., and Pine, G.J. *The Counselor in the Schools: A Reconceptualization.* Boston: Houghton Mifflin Company, 1968.

Bradford, L.P.; Gibb, J.R.; and Benne, K.D. "Two Educational Innovations." In *T-Group Theory and Laboratory Method,* edited by L.P. Bradford et al., pp. 1-15. New York: John Wiley and Sons, Inc., 1964.

Breger, L., and McGaugh, J.L. "Another View of Behavior Therapy." In *Sources of Gain in Counseling and Psychotherapy,* New York: Holt, Rinehart and Winston, 1967. edited by B.G. Berenson and R.R. Carkhuff, pp. 323-357.

Buchheimer, A.; Goodman, I.; and Sircus, G. "Videotapes and Kine-scopic Recordings as Situational Test and Laboratory Exercises in Empathy for the Training of Counselors." N.D.E.A. Title VII Research Project, No. 7-42-0550-1670. 1965.

Caplan, G. "Types of Mental Health Consultation." Paper delivered at meeting. Los Angeles, March, 1961.

Coffey, H.S. "Socio and Psyche Group Process: Integrative Concepts." In *Perspectives on the Group Process,* edited by C.G. Kemp, pp. 46-56. Boston: Houghton, Mifflin & Company, 1964.

Cohn, B. et al. "Group Counseling: An Orientation." *Personnel and Guidance Journal* 42 (1963):355-358.

Cohn, Ruth C. "Living - Learning Encounters: The Theme-Centered Interactional Method." Mimeograph. 1969.

Cohn, Ruth C. "The Theme-Centered Interactional Method: Group Therapists as Group Educators." *Journal of Group Psychoanalysis and Process* 2 (1970):19-36.

Cohn, Ruth C. "Style and Spirit of the Theme-Centered Interactional Method." In *Progress in Group and Family Therapy,* edited by Helen S. Kaplan and C.J. Sager, pp. 852-878. New York: Brunner, Mazel, 1972.

Dole, A.A. "Client Quest - A Key to Counseling." *Personnel and Guidance Journal* 45 (1967):455-463.

Dreyfus, E.A. "Humanness: A Therapeutic Variable." *Personnel and Guidance Journal* 45 (1967):573-578.

Driver, Helen I., et al. *Counseling and Learning Through Small Group Discussion.* Madison, Wisc.: Monona Publications, 1962.

Durkin, Helen E. *The Group in Depth.* New York: International Universities Press, 1964.

Ellis, A. *Reason and Emotion in Psychotherapy.* New York: Lyle Stuart, 1962.

212

Foulkes, S.H. and Anthony, E.J. *Group Psychotherapy.* Baltimore, Penguin Books, 1965.

Freud, S. *Group Psychology and the Analysis of the Ego.* New York: Liverwright, 1949.

Fullmer, D., and Bernard, H.W. *Counseling: Content and Process.* Chicago: Science Research Associates, 1964.

Garwood, Dorothy S. "The Significance and Dynamics of Sensitivity Training Programs." *International Journal of Group Psychotherapy* 17 (1967):457-473.

Gazda, G.M. and Folds, J.H. *Group Guidance: A Critical Incidents Approach.* Follett Educational Corp., 1968.

Gibb, J.R., and Gibb, L.M. "Humanistic Elements in Group Growth." In *Challenges of Humanistic Psychology,* edited by F.F.T. Bugental. New York: McGraw-Hill, 1967.

Ginott, H.G. *Group Psychotherapy with Children.* New York: McGraw-Hill, 1961.

Glanz, E.C. *Groups in Guidance: The Dynamics of Groups and the Application of Groups in Guidance.* Boston: Allyn and Bacon, Inc., 1962.

Goldman, L. "Group Guidance: Content and Process." *Personnel and Guidance Journal* 40 (1962):518-522.

Gordon, M., and Liberman, N. "Group Psychotherapy: Being and Becoming." *Personnel and Guidance Journal* 49 (1971):611-618.

Hahn, M. *Psychoevaluation: Adaptation, Distribution, Adjustment.* New York: McGraw-Hill, 1963.

Heath, R. *The Reasonable Adventurer.* Pittsburgh: University of Pittsburgh Press, 1964.

Hummel, R.C. "Ego Counseling in Guidance." In *Guidance, An Examination,* edited by R.L. Mosher et al., pp. 82-110. New York: Harcourt, Brace and World, Inc., 1965.

Johnson, E.L. "Existentialism, Self Theory and the Existential Self." *Personnel and Guidance Journal* 46 (1967):53-59.

Jones, R.M. *Fantasy and Feeling in Education.* New York: New York University Press, 1968.

Journad, S.M. "Counseling for Healthy Personality." In *Counseling for the Liberal Arts Campus,* edited by J.C. Heston and W.B. Frick, pp. 72-90. Yellow Springs, Ohio: The Antioch Press, 1968.

Kadis, Asya L.; Krasner, J.; et al. *A Practicum of Group Psychotherapy.* New York: Harper and Row, 1963.

Katz, E., and Lazarsfeld, P.F. *Personal Influence.* Gelncoe, Ill: The Free Press, 1955.

Kelman, H.C. "The Role of the Group in the Induction of Therapeutic Change." *International Journal of Group Psychotherapy* 13 (1963):399-432.

Knowles, R.T., and Barr, D.J. "Pseudo-Subjectivity in Counseling." *Personnel and Guidance Journal* 46 (1968):572-579.

Krumbeltz, J.D. "Promoting Adaptive Behavior: New Answers to Familiar Questions." In *Revolution in Counseling,* edited by J.D. Krumbeltz, pp. 3-27. Boston: Houghton Mifflin Company, 1966.

Lakin, M. and Dobbs, W.H. "The Therapy Group Promotes an Hypothesis of Psychogenesis: A Study in Group Process." *International Journal of Group Psychotherapy* 12 (1962):64-75.

Lifton, W.M. *Working with Groups.* New York: John Wiley and Sons, Inc., 1967.

Marsh, L.C. "Group Treatment of the Psychoses by the Psychological Equivalent of the Revival." *Mental Hygiene* 15 (1931):328-349.

Maslow, A. *Toward a Psychology of Being.* Princeton, N.J.:Van Nostrand, 1962.

McDaniel, H.B. "Counseling Perspectives: Old and New." In *Revolution in Counseling,* edited by J.D. Krumboltz, pp. 79-95. Boston: Houghton Mifflin Company, 1966.

McGowan, J.F. "Counseling's Social Response." In *Psychology and the Problems of Society,* edited by F.K. Korten; S.W. Cook; and J.T. Lacey, pp. 67-73. Washington, D.C.: American Psychological Association, 1970.

Menninger, K.A. *Theory of Psychoanalytic Technique,* New York: Basic Books, 1958.

Miles, M.B. "The T-Group and the Classroom." In *T-Group Theory and Laboratory Method,* edited by L.P. Bradford, et al., pp. 452-457. New York: John Wiley and Sons, 1964.

Murphy, G. "Group Psychotherapy in our Society." In *Group Psychotherapy and Group Function,* edited by M. Rosenbaum and M. Berger, pp. 33-42. New York: Basic Books, Inc., 1963.

Orton, J.W. *Readings in Group Work.* New York: Selected Academic Readings, 1964.

Patterson, C.H. *Theories of Counseling and Psychotherapy.* New York: Harper and Row, 1966.

Pierson, G.A. "Counselor Education in Regular Session Institutes." U.S. Department of Health, Education and Welfare. Contract No. OE3-99-088. 1965.

Postgraduate Center for Mental Health, Community Mental Health Department Courses 1003 and 904, 1960.

Postman, N. and Weingartner, C. *Teaching as a Subversive Activity.* New York: Delacorte Press, 1969.

Rogers, C.R. "The Necessary and Sufficient Conditions of Therapeutic Personality Change." *Journal of Consulting Psychology* 21 (1957):95-103

Rogers, C.R. *Carl Rogers on Encounter Groups.* New York: Harper and Row, 1970.

Sachs, B.M. *The Student, the Interview, and the Curriculum.* Boston: Houghton Mifflin Company, 1966.

Samler, J. "The School and Self-Understanding." In *Guidance and*

Examination, edited by R.L. Mosher, pp. 174-192. New York: Harcourt, Brace and World, Inc., 1965.

Sanford, N. *The American College,* pp. 253-283. New York: John Wiley and Sons, 1962.

Satir, V.W. *Conjoint Family Therapy.* Palo Alto: Science and Behavior Books, Inc., 1964.

Scheidlinger, S. "The Relationship of Group Therapy to other Group Influence Attempts." In *Group Psychotherapy and Group Function,* edited by M. Rosenbaum and M. Berger, pp. 352-362. New York: Basic Books, 1963.

Shoben, E.J. Jr. "The Counseling Experience as Personal Development." *Personnel and Guidance Journal* 44 (1965):224-230.

Slavson, S.R. *An Introduction to Group Therapy.* New York: International Universities Press, 1943.

Slavson, S.R. *A Textbook in Analytic Group Psychotherapy.* New York: International Universities Press, 1964.

Strickland, B. "Kierkegaard and Counseling for Individuality." *Personnel and Guidance Journal* 44 (1966):470-474.

Sullivan, H.S. *The Psychiatric Interview.* New York: W.W. Norton & Co., 1954.

Thorne, F.C. *Principles of Personality Counseling,* Brandon, Vermont: Journal of Clinical Psychology Press, 1950.

Tiedemann, D.V. and Field, F.L. "Guidance: The Science of Purposeful Action Applied Through Education," In *Guidance, an Examination,* edited by R.L. Mosher, et al., pp. 192-194. New York: Harcourt, Brace and World, Inc., 1965.

Wolberg, L.R. *The Technique of Psychotherapy.* New York: Grune and Stratton, 1967.

Wolf, E.K. and Wolf, A. *Psychoanalysis in Groups: The Mystique of Group Dynamics.* Topical Problems of Psychotherapy vol. 2, pp. 119-154. New York: Karger, Basel, 1960.

Wrenn, C.G. "Two Psychological Worlds: An Attempted Rapprochement." In *Revolution in Counseling,* edited by J.D. Krumboltz, pp. 95-107. Boston: Houghton Mifflin Company, 1966.

Wrenn, C.G. "The Culturally Encapsulated Counselor." In *Guidance, an Examination,* edited by R.L. Mosher et al., pp. 214-255. New York: Harcourt, Brace and World, Inc., 1965.

Zaccaria, J.S. "Developmental Tasks: Implications for the Goals of Guidance." *Personnel and Guidance Journal* 44 (1965):372-375.

Zinberg, N.E. and Friedman, L.J. "Problems in Working with Dynamic Groups." *International Journal of Group Psychotherapy* 17 (1967):451-457.

Index

[1]These processes are also illustrated and described in the cassettes and accompanying notes available separately from the publisher.